The Romanesque Abbey of St Peter at Gloucester

This volume is dedicated to the masons who built St Peter's Abbey in the 11th and 12th centuries, and to the past and present masons of Gloucester Cathedral whose skills have contributed to keeping this wonderful building alive into the 21st century

The Romanesque Abbey
of St Peter at Gloucester

(Gloucester Cathedral)

Carolyn Heighway
and
Richard Bryant

with
Malcolm Thurlby

 OXBOW | books
Oxford & Philadelphia

Published in the United Kingdom in 2020 by
OXBOW BOOKS
The Old Music Hall, 106–108 Cowley Road, Oxford, OX4 1JE

and in the United States by
OXBOW BOOKS
1950 Lawrence Road, Havertown, PA 19083

Paperback Edition: ISBN 978-1-78925-414-3
Digital Edition: ISBN 978-1-78925-415-0 (epub)

A CIP record for this book is available from the British Library

Library of Congress Control Number:2019951279

Designed and typeset by Past Historic, Kings Stanley, Gloucestershire
Cover design by Declan Ingram

Printed in the United Kingdom by Short Run Press

For a complete list of Oxbow titles, please contact:

UNITED KINGDOM
Oxbow Books
Telephone (01865) 241249
Email: oxbow@oxbowbooks.com
www.oxbowbooks.com

UNITED STATES OF AMERICA
Oxbow Books
Telephone (800) 791-9354, Fax (610) 853-9146
Email: queries@casemateacademic.com
www.casemateacademic.com/oxbow

Oxbow Books is part of the Casemate Group

Front cover: The Romanesque nave arcade looking south from the north aisle.
Back cover: General view from the north-east of Gloucester Cathedral, showing the eastern arm.

Contents

List of illustrations

ix

Photographic credits

Unattributed photographs are by Carolyn Heighway or Richard Bryant. Skycell photograph by permission of Gloucester Cathedral. Other photographs are indicated by initials as follows:-

AFK Anthony Feltham-King

AH Angelo Hornak

CH Chiz Harward

MT Malcolm Thurlby

RA Richard Auckland

RD Rita Dawe

RKM Richard Morriss

OC Oliver Chamberlain

WD William Douglas

Drawing credits

Unless otherwise stated the drawings are by Richard Bryant, often using photogrammetric and plan surveys as a base.

Preface

I retired as archaeological consultant of Gloucester Cathedral in 2009; I had held the post for nearly thirty years.

During that time I realised just how much remains of the Romanesque abbey, and how remarkable is its survival. In 2001 it became clear that the new survey being prepared by Cartographical Surveys could be used to map very precisely the outline of the Romanesque building. Originally we envisaged a plan only, and this was produced by our daughter Gemma. Later, since the survey was on four levels and included OD levels, Gemma produced an outline, three-dimensional version (Heighway 2008, fig3).

My husband Richard Bryant joined the project in 2012: in that year he finished his work on the *Corpus of Anglo-Saxon Stone Sculpture: vol X Western Midlands*. He undertook to reconstruct elevations using the available data. We were able to overlay the electronic plans, compare them, and combine information from the photogrammetric elevations. He has also contributed extensively to the text. He produced the reconstruction (**128**).

We circulated 25 copies of the 'pre-publication draft' to various colleagues, which prompted some intriguing and diverse debate and resulted in much re-writing. We were also able to incorporate some information from excavations carried out by Border Archaeology for Project Pilgrim in 2017.

We are very grateful to our friend and colleague, Malcolm Thurlby, who has contributed a valuable chapter on the sources, parallels and wider context for Romanesque Gloucester abbey.

Carolyn Heighway
Canon Emeritus of Gloucester Cathedral
Petertide 2019

Acknowledgements

Carolyn was privileged to know Bernard Ashwell (cathedral architect 1960-1985), whose devotion to the cathedral included fabric surveys long before these became a required component of repair projects. Since then Basil Comely (1985-1998), Ian Stainburn (1998-2009), Antony Feltham-King (2010 to the present) have generously contributed their time, their knowledge, and sometimes their photographs. Neil Birdsall, architect to Tewkesbury abbey from 1978 to 2010, not only shared various insights but took us into the Tewkesbury abbey roof spaces where we were able to measure in the western towers.

Arthur Price, an authority on the quarrying of stone and of masons, has been generous with his time and his information, in spite of being a busy farmer.

Michael Hare, honorary research fellow at Bristol University, has been an indefatigable and acute critic as well as a valued friend.

We are grateful to other colleagues who have responded to our draft publication in 2017: Susan Hamilton, Malcolm Thurlby, Richard Gem, Eric Fernie, and John Rhodes; also to John McNeill and Richard Plant who toured the cathedral roof spaces with us in 2017 and made valuable observations. John Rhodes started us on a reconsideration of the complex development of the south transept — we are particularly grateful for his comments.

The cathedral staff have always been helpful, especially Nicholas Hilyer, Dean's Verger, and the many volunteer guides. The Canon Chancellor, Celia Thomson, is to be commended for her patience especially on our last visit to the roof. Pascal Mychalysin, Master Mason, has a profound knowledge of stone-types and of the archaeology of the whole building. The diocesan officers in Church House, including diocesan secretary Benjamin Preece-Smith, cheerfully allowed us to measure the windows of their office and visit their roof.

We are grateful to Anne Cranston, project manager of Project Pilgrim, to Richard Morriss, the present cathedral archaeologist, and to Chiz Harward of Urban Archaeology, all of whom helped provide pre-publication information on the 2017 excavations.

Heartfelt thanks to Susan Hamilton for undertaking copy-editing and saving us from many errors. Any that remain are our responsiblility.

Some of those who made considerable contributions to the Romanesque story are no longer with us. Steve Bagshaw recorded the archaeology at Gloucester Cathedral from about 2002 for three years, and Richard Keith Morris produced an invaluable survey of the worked stone in 2001. We still miss their enthusiasm and insight.

INTRODUCTION

The abbey church of St Peter at Gloucester was begun by Abbot Serlo in 1089 **(1)**. Its eastern arm, crossing and transepts were probably complete by the dedication ceremony of 15 July 1100;[1] the nave is usually assumed to have been built in the early decades of the 12th century.[2] A new nave vault in the 13th century was followed in the 14th by a remarkable conversion of the building, instigated by the abbey after the burial there of Edward II, and carried out largely by adaption of the existing fabric (Hamilton 2011). There followed a 15th-century tower, and a late 15th-century Lady Chapel. After the Reformation in 1542 the abbey was converted to a cathedral (Hoyle 2011, 53-4).

However, because of the nature of the 14th-

1 General view from the north-east of Gloucester Cathedral, showing the eastern arm. *MT*

1 Wilson 1980, 128. The date may have been chosen to commemorate the first anniversary of the fall of Jerusalem: Hare 2002.
2 The main source for this and other building dates is the late 14th century abbey *Historia:* Hart 1863, 3-125, cited in the present volume using the translation by Barber (1988). There are a few mentions in other chronicles

(Heighway 2003, 27). The dearth of written evidence means that the building itself is a primary source. It has had many commentators: eg Fernie 2000, 157-60, Thurlby 1985a, Wilson 1980 and 1985, and references cited in all three.

century adaption, a considerable part of the Romanesque fabric remains. Serlo's crypt survives almost in its entirety. The choir above retains the original galleries, including gallery chapels above the transeptal chapels, and the original choir internal elevation is discernible behind the 14th-century re-facing, though the apsidal east end and the upper walls were destroyed. The transepts are essentially Romanesque in plan but their internal elevations were refaced in the 14th century when large windows were inserted. The nave with its lofty pillars survives almost in its original form, although the present vault was added and the clerestory windows modified in the 13th and 14th centuries. The western two bays were entirely rebuilt in the 15th century.[3] The nave north aisle retains its Romanesque rib vaulting, with windows only slightly modified in the medieval period. The south aisle, rebuilt from 1318, nevertheless still retains its Romanesque responds and capitals.

A hallmark of Serlo's church is the simplicity of the eastern arm. Openings are outlined by a simple roll which rises from a base but carries no capitals; blind openings also have continuous rolls with bases but without capitals. Wilson (1985, 58) regards these as key to the work of the 'Gloucester Master'. Soffits are mostly plain; pairs of half-shafts with plain cushion capitals flank the entrances to the transeptal chapels and are used on the crossing piers. There may have been some nook shafts (pp33-4). Chevron ornament in the crypt was added slightly later. The chevron and other decoration on the south transept may not have been part of the original build: if it was then it represents a departure from the overall restraint of the eastern arm (below pp43-4).

The present study was inspired by the availability of two sources of information.

Firstly, there are accurate plans on four levels (crypt, ground, triforium, and roof, including OD levels) commissioned by the then Cathedral architect Ian Stainburn and carried out by Cartographical Surveys Ltd in March 2001. These plans can be overlaid and compared at any scale and provide a high level of accuracy and detail surpassing the previous 19th-century plans (Carter and Basire 1807; Britton 1829; Waller 1856; Waller 1890).

Secondly, there has been a series of photogrammetric surveys carried out by various agencies since 1994. These provide scaled elevations related to OD levels against which elements of the Romanesque elevations may be calibrated.

Initially our aim was to provide only ground plans, but as study and observation continued, it became apparent that the information was available to draw elevations as well. It is true there are no recent accurate elevations of the interior (the relative rarity of internal repairs means this has not been financially justified) and it has been beyond our resources to carry out any major interior survey work. Nevertheless, the 19th-century elevations can be used (Carter and Basire 1807; Britton 1829) and checked by using readings taken with a digital measuring instrument and by extrapolating OD levels through apertures (usually windows).

Our aim then became, not only to provide accurate plans of the Romanesque church (**2, 3, 4, 5**), but also to reconstruct some of the missing parts of this truly remarkable building, using the surveys as well as archaeological records.[4]

---

3 Date from Leland's 16th-century account: 'These notable things I learned of an ould man lately a Monke of Gloucester….Abbot Morwent newly erected the very West End of the Church and 2 Arches of the Body of the Church, one on each side…' Toulmin-Smith, vol 2, part v, p61.

4 Reports prefixed GCAR are in the Cathedral archives; many are available online. See www.bgas.org.uk/publications/gcar.

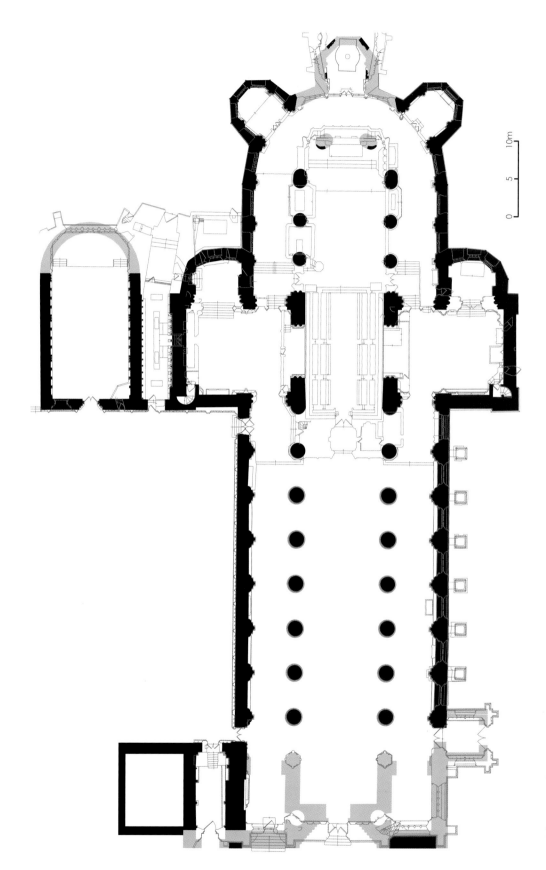

2 The ground-plan of the Romanesque abbey church, superimposed on the modern plan, from the 2001 survey.

3

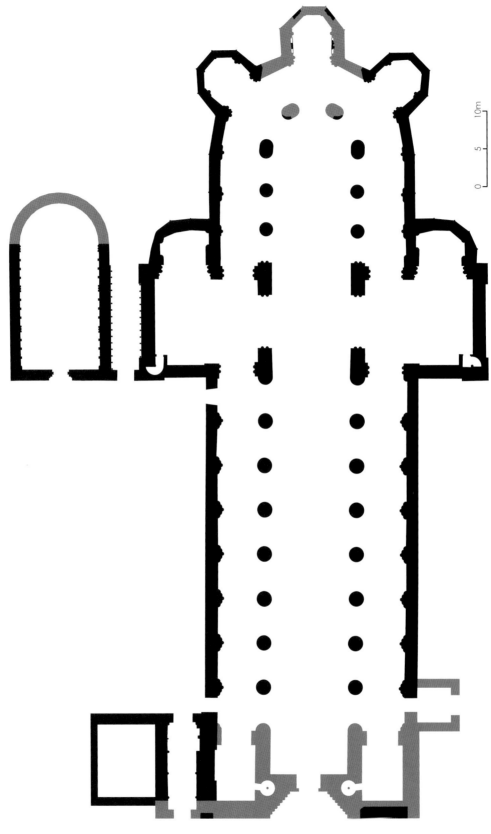

3 The ground plan of the Romanesque abbey church. Shaded parts of the plan are reconstructed. Details of the eastern axial chapel and the foundations of the west front were observed by the authors during archaeological excavations in 2017. The recessed west entrance is derived from the plan of Tewkesbury Abbey. *Drawing: R Bryant and G Fowlie.*

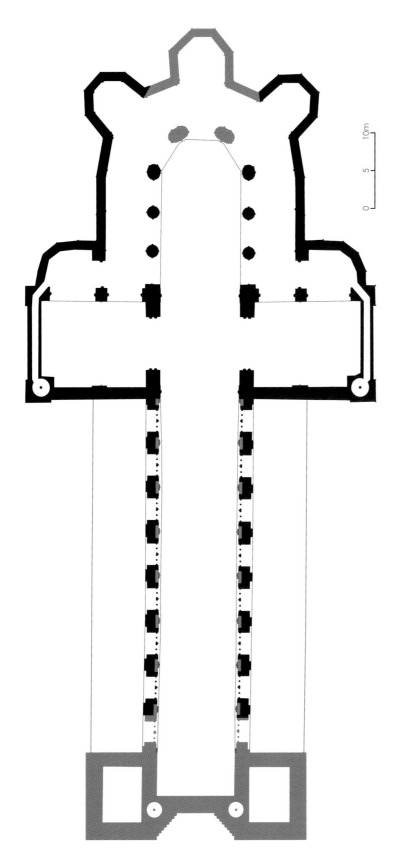

4 The tribune/triforium plan of the Romanesque abbey, based on the 2001 survey. Shaded parts of the plan are reconstructed. For a plan of the elliptical piers around the eastern apse at a larger scale, see **17** and **18**.

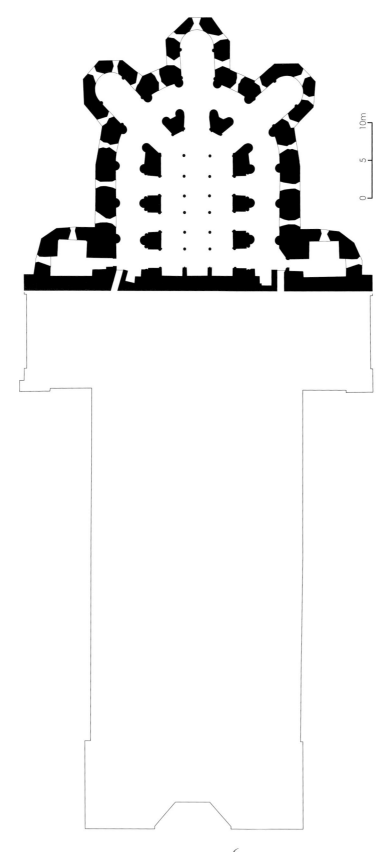

5 Plan of the crypt as it was in the early 12th century after the piers had been enlarged and the ambulatory vaulting reinforced with ribs and additional transverse arches. Based on the 2001 survey.

10m

5

0

THE EASTERN ARM

The crypt

Serlo's crypt under the eastern arm had three bays and a polygonal apse, an ambulatory, three radiating apsidal chapels, and chapels to north and south underlying the eastern chapels of the transepts above. The floor level of the central vessel was lower than the surrounding ambulatory.[1] The plan (**5**) delineates the work as it was by the early 12th century and does not attempt to reproduce the thoroughly-encased late 11th-century work for which the clearest presentation is still F S Waller's coloured drawing (**6**).

The present entrance to the crypt is in the south transept but there was originally a corresponding entrance to the north. The entrance-way and remains of the northern stair can still be seen from inside the crypt.

The central vessel has groin vaulting supported

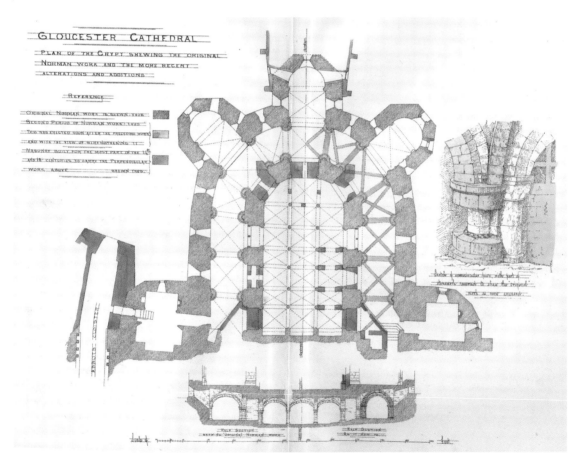

6 The phases of the crypt as drawn by F S Waller (1876) (north to the left).

1 The reason is unknown; the same is true of the choir above. The holes around the piers of the central vessel were first excavated before 1855, re-excavated in 1941-3, and reinforced in 1971: Heighway 2003, 32.

7 The central vessel of the crypt with inset detail of decorated volute capital. The holes around the piers to expose the bases and plinths were made in the mid 19th century. *WD*

8 Volute capital with moustached head, in the crypt. *AH*

9 Volute capital in the central vessel of the crypt.

10 View of the west end of the crypt (when used as the stone store) showing the variety of capitals (volute, cushion, scallop) and one of the original bases.

by half-shaft responds and two rows of columns (**7, 8, 9**). The columns have simple bulbous bases set on square plinths[2] and most have volute capitals some of which have vertical rectangular panels in the centre of each face. Three of these panels are carved — two have foliate decoration and one a face with a flamboyant moustache (**7, 8**). One of the columns near the west end has a cushion capital and the responds have scallop capitals (**10**).

The crypt ambulatory (**11**) originally had transverse arches, the bays between being groin-vaulted. The transverse and arcade arches were supported by half-round columns, all of similar size. Some movement must have taken place, so that reinforcement was necessary. The ambulatory piers were enlarged by enveloping them in new masonry to create larger cylinders, the transverse arches were strengthened by inserting beneath them another arch (sometimes carrying chevron ornament), and the groins were underpinned by new ribs.[3]

2 The bases and plinths are most clearly visible at the west end.

3 Waller (**6**) did not colour in the additional strengthening of the vaults in the north ambulatory, presumably because he wanted to demonstrate the original form of the vault on the northern half of the drawing.

11 The crypt south ambulatory looking west. *AH*

The use of chevron (**12**) has led to the assumption that this work took place in the early 12th century though it could have been earlier (Welander 1991, 30). (A row of chevron appears above panels of blind arcading in the south-eastern chapel (**13**) but the arcading and chevron are clearly inserted.)

Wilson thought that the crypt arcade wall had sunk about 40cm more on the south than on the north (Wilson 1985, 69). The south ambulatory wall leans outwards, by about 10cm at wall-plate level, and the south-east transept gallery chapel wall leans out even more, by 20cm. However the levels of the original late 11th century

abaci (those few still accessible) of the crypt ambulatory arcade vary in height AOD by only a few centimetres.[4] Moreover in the eastern arm as a whole the external Romanesque string courses are level.[5] All this suggests that the problem in the crypt was not the differential sinking of the foundations but outward movement threatening the failure of the crypt (and higher?) vaults.[6]

4 Measuring from the top of original abacus, where exposed, to the known floor levels. Heights in m. OD of two abaci on north side: 14.56; 14.61. Heights in m. OD of three on south side: 14.69; 14.7; 14.72.
5 Photogrammetric surveys in 2000 and 2018.
6 This is not to deny the seriousness of structural movement at Gloucester: the nave south aisle wall leaned out so severely it had to be rebuilt in 1318, and both the south-east turret of the south transept and the north-east

12 The crypt, view south from east ambulatory showing reinforcing arches with chevron decoration. *AH*

13 The crypt, south-eastern chapel showing inserted arcade of arches with chevron decoration. *WD*

This would have become apparent as the upper storeys of the choir were built. It could have been corrected even before the 1100 dedication when the eastern arm and transepts are supposed to have been complete (Wilson 1980, 128).[7]

turret of the north transept lean out 40cm at the top. When the south transept was altered in the 1330s the south wall of the crossing tower also leaned out; it had to be cut back in order to receive new, correctly vertical, shafts. Strengthening in the crypt in the 14th century was greater on the south side than on the north and the same is true of the south tribune gallery.

7 Excavations in 2017 for a lift-pit in the north ambulatory exposed a deep crack 3-5cm wide in the underlying vault infilling, sealed by the trample for the north ambulatory wall superstructure, which suggests that the structural failure may have begun at an early stage (inf. C Harward).

The choir, ambulatory and tribune gallery

The plan of the choir (**3, 4**) mirrors the crypt below (**5**) and the design has been called 'among the most idiosyncratic … of the late 11th century' (Wilson 1980, 128). The choir had three straight bays and an apse, with an arcaded ambulatory (**14**) and arcaded gallery above (**15**): the arcades are still visible behind the 14th-century choir facing (**16**). The gallery arcade arches carried hood-mouldings.[8]

The squat cylindrical columns forming the arcade were unusually widely spaced; and in order to maintain the same spacing in the eastern bays of the apse the four columns here were slightly elliptical in plan rather than circular (**3, 4, 17**).[9] The gallery arcade was even more eccentric. The

14 South ambulatory of the choir looking east. *AH*

8 The tribune level columns are set back slightly from the corresponding columns below, so that when the ground floor arcade was cut back by a whole order during the 14th-century refacing of the choir, the gallery arcade lost only a small amount of its outer order. As a result some traces of the tribune gallery level hood mouldings have survived, especially on the north side (**15**). The ground floor arches possibly also carried hood-mouldings.

9 The two central eastern columns were removed in the 14th century to accommodate the extension east of the choir; the outlines of part of their bases were recorded during excavation in 1867 (Welander 1991, 178). The eastern axial chapels on both levels, removed when the late 15th-century Lady Chapel was built, can be reconstructed from the surviving chapel in the crypt below, and remains of the side-walls of the apse were found during archaeological investigations prior to reflooring in 2017.

12

15 North tribune gallery looking east. *AH*

chord piers, though partly cut away to make way for the 14th-century work, survive well enough to show that their east-west axis is actually not as elongated as the pier below them. Therefore, in order to maintain arches of equal size to those in the straight bays, the two eastern columns have to be even more elongated than those below (**4, 18**).[10]

At gallery level there are single, slightly flat-

10 The only alternative interpretation is that the gallery piers were the same size as those below and that the three apse tribune arches were slightly wider and higher than the others.

tened half-shafts (diameter *c*.28cm) on each cardinal face of the drum columns (**15**). Each shaft represents the soffit of an arch above. One shaft faces towards the tribune gallery and 'supports' the quadrant or half-barrel arch of the vault; shafts to west and east visually support the inner order of the arcade arch. On each column a shaft also faced inward towards the choir; the shaft was sliced off to take the 14th-century facings. Of these inward-facing shafts, one (*c*. 25cm wide) has survived on the chord column on the north side (**19**): the shaft is slightly east of centre which suggests that it was originally one of

13

16 The choir, part of the north side, showing Romanesque arches visible behind 14th-century facing. The cut-back hood mouldings above the tribune arcade arches are arrowed. *MT*

a pair (**18**).[11] These shafts are assumed to represent the position of vault arches (Thurlby 1985a, 47; Wilson 1985, 63) and are the principal evidence for the existence of a stone vault of some kind in the choir.

The chord gallery piers each carried two shafts on the ambulatory side (**20**), and presumably the missing elongated piers at the eastern end

11 Wilson (1985, 70) reconstructed this as one of three. The corresponding ovoid pier on the south is slightly different in both shape and alignment, so the shaft here has not survived.

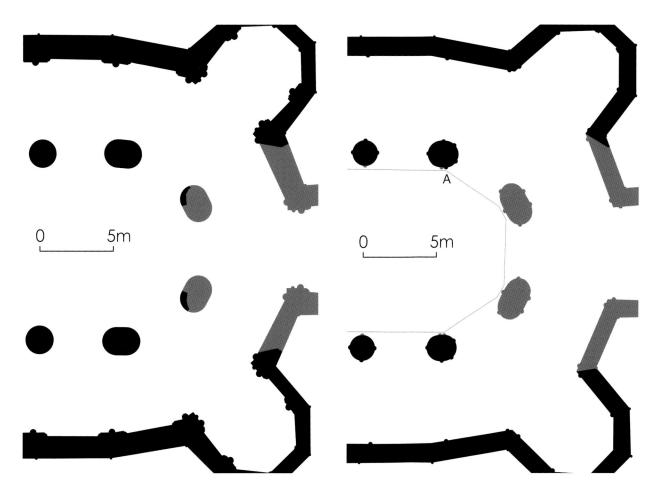

17 Detail of the plan of the east ambulatory, showing (in black) surviving features, together with segments of the foundations for the two elliptical eastern piers that were found in 1872. Destroyed parts of these piers, and the eastern chapel, have been reconstructed and are shown in grey tone.

18 Detail of the plan of the tribune gallery east end, showing surviving features in black and the reconstructed elliptical piers in grey tone. At this level the chord piers are not as elongated as their ground floor counterparts. Only one of the half-round vaulting shafts has survived on the inner faces of the arcade piers (labelled A on the plan, with all the other inner-face shafts shown in grey tone). The position of this surviving shaft suggests that it was one of a pair, probably supporting a double roll-moulding on the vaulting arch on the chord of the apse.

also carried two shafts, in which case the missing vault of the eastern end of the gallery can be reconstructed with reasonable certainty (**21, 22**).

Externally the walls of ambulatory and gallery survive, often to their full height (the wall-plate was raised in the 14th century in order to lower the roof pitch and hence make room for clerestory windows) (**23**). The corbel-table of the ambulatories is still visible in one bay of the north-east chapel (**24, 25**); it consists of a plain chamfered string course above a row of corbels about 35cm apart with undercut faces decorated

with little barrels. The top of the corbels is at 27.6m AOD; the top of the chamfered string course above was at 27.8m.[12]

The height of the Romanesque corbel-table of

12 The corresponding corbel table on the south ambulatory elevation is visible as a course with square stones at 35cm intervals where the corbels have been chopped off or replaced.

15

20 The north face of the northern chord pier in the tribune gallery looking south-west, showing two half shafts.

19 View from south side of choir tribune gallery to the north, showing vaulting shaft surviving on the chord of the apse embedded in 14th-century masonry. *MT*

the choir, and presumably of transepts and nave, can be estimated at 36m AOD.[13] We have assumed its form was the same as that of the ambulatory.

Though our information on the ground floor and tribune gallery is plentiful (except for windows, discussed below) the clerestory and high vault have generated much debate.

In situ survivals of the upper part of the choir
An important external remnant of the Romanesque choir survives *in situ*, a section of blind arcading close to the tower on the north side (**26**). The arcade had a string-course above and below and arches with simple outlined roll and bases but no capitals. Each arch measures *c.*43cm

---

13 There are various indications of the height of the corbel-table.
(i) The sill of the door in the south-east turret which originally opened onto the south transept roof leads must be a few centimetres above the height of the transept wall-head (Wilson 1985, 70-71); the sill level is 36.2m AOD.
(ii) An analysis of the masonry inside the nave roof space (Bagshaw 2002a, 4) established that the 12th-century masonry of the nave survives to its greatest height at the east end of the north clerestory at 35.7m AOD. (iii) The top of the surviving strip buttresses on the nave clerestory (**76**) is at 35.5 AOD. (iv) The base of the round corner turret surviving in the north-

east angle of choir and north transept (**25**), at 35.5m AOD, has one stone integral with the north face of the choir north wall masonry, so at this level there was still a choir wall to which it was bonded. (The top of the 12th-century nave wall is visible in the nave roof space, next to the remains of the round turret (**69**), confirming that the tower turret base extended below the top of the wall.) (v) The string course at the base of the upper decorated portions of the early-12th century transept turrets is at 36m AOD.

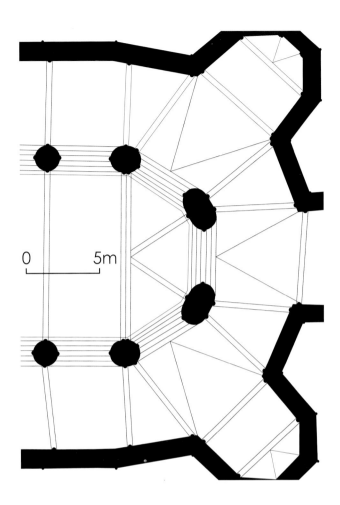

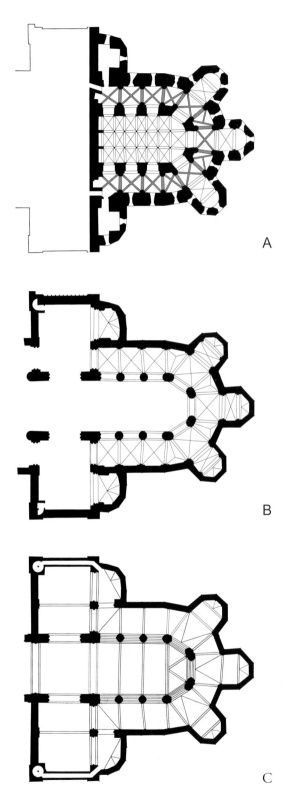

21 Plan of the east end at tribune level, showing the surviving vaulting of the gallery and chapels, together with a reconstruction of the main transverse arches of the central vessel and of the vaulting of the apse and eastern gallery.

22 Plans of crypt (A), ground floor (B) and tribune gallery (C) showing existing and reconstructed vaulting: a barrel vault in the choir is assumed.

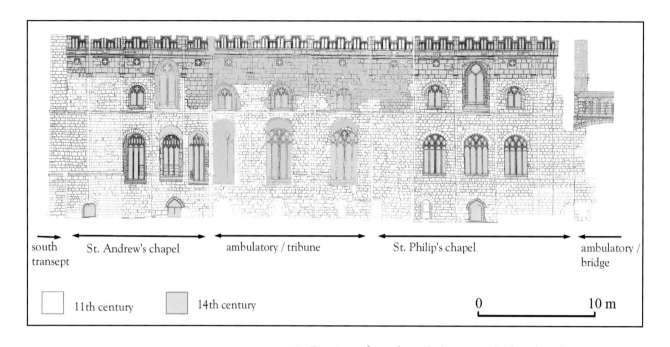

south transept ← → St. Andrew's chapel ← → ambulatory / tribune ← → St. Philip's chapel ← → ambulatory / bridge

☐ 11th century   ☐ 14th century

0 ———— 10 m

23 Exterior of south ambulatory and chapels: photogrammetric elevations with added phasing (Bagshaw 2000, fig4). The diagram shows that the window in the tribune chapel above that of St Andrew, which is decorated with ball-flower, could not have been built until after the raising of the ambulatory walls. (St Philip's chapel is more often known as St Thomas').

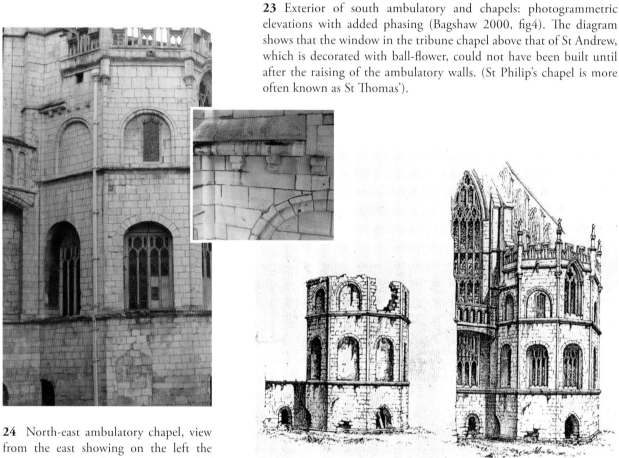

24 North-east ambulatory chapel, view from the east showing on the left the surviving length of Romanesque corbel table. Inset detail *CH*

25 F S Waller's drawing of the same chapel (Waller 1856, fig 13).

18

26 View south from the north ambulatory roof, showing the fragment of blind arcading; also the base of the overhanging circular turret surviving from the Romanesque tower.

wide, and 95cm high from base to apex of arch.[14] A remnant of another shaft of an arcade is visible on the adjacent transept (**27**), showing that the east face of the transept was similarly decorated. The east face of the south transept probably also carried blind arcading.[15]

14 There was at the time of writing no photogrammetric survey of this part of the choir. The drawing of the blind arcade (e.g. **32, 34, 36**) has been constructed by following masonry courses round from the photogrammetric survey of the closely adjacent north transept.

15 A remnant of what may be the basal string-course of the blind arcade (**61**) survives on a buttress representing the remains of the Romanesque clerestory wall (Wilson 1985, 71), though the string-course is 25cm too low according to our calculations.

27 The fragment of blind arcading, viewed from the east towards the west, showing its presence on the north transept east face.

A similarly-placed but larger arcade is to be seen on the transepts at Tewkesbury abbey (**89**).

Evidence from the transepts (below, p. 35) indicates the strong possibility that there was a high-level passage in the thickness of the walls of the choir at a level of 30.7m AOD.

There are also other Romanesque fragments, not *in situ* but re-used, which may be from the missing parts of the choir. The most significant of these can be seen in the tribune gallery, reused as responds for subsidiary arches.[16] Three columns carrying scallop and cushion capitals are made up of six monolithic shafts (**28**).[17] The shaft diameter is 29.5cm (10cm larger than the columns in the nave triforium); the longest shaft section is 98cm. These monolithic shafts have been seen as deriving from a high-level passage at the east end (see below).

A stone vault

The half-shafts on the faces of the gallery piers suggest there was a stone vault of some kind

16 They were re-used here in the 12th century (Wilson 1985, 71) or in the 14th century (McAleer 1986, 157).

17 The sections range in length from 91.4m to 48.3m; circumference 92.7cm (diameter 29.5cm).

(above p14). It is worth noting that the space to be vaulted in the choir is exactly the same dimension as the early 12th century chapter house, which has a slightly pointed barrel vault (**101**; **3** for plan). The chapter house vault has transverse arches with soffit roll mouldings; at the chord of the apse is a respond with paired half-shafts topped by a scalloped capital supporting an arch with a double soffit roll (**100**). The choir vault could have had similar arches, whether the vault was a groin or barrel. As it happens, there is, reused on the choir north exterior, a capital of the right size for the chord capital; it is a triple scallop originally 0.77m wide and 1.17m deep, reused at the base of a 14th-century flying buttress (McAleer 1986, 170) (**29, 30**). There is also, reused on a buttress on the south choir clerestory, a considerable length of voussoirs with paired soffit rolls (each roll 24cm diameter) which could have come from the chord arch of the choir (**31**).

28 Monolithic shafts, possibly from the Romanesque choir elevation, re-used in the tribune gallery.

29 Part of a capital with three scallops re-used as a buttress base on the north side of the 14th-century choir.

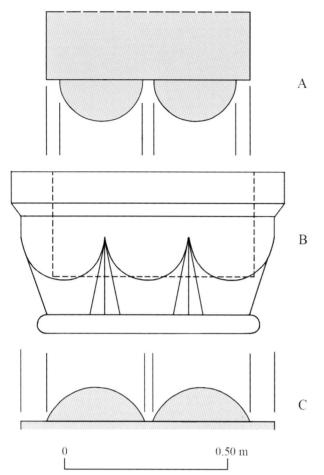

0   0.50 m

A

B

C

30
(A): Section of double soffit roll re-used in 14th century on the underside of a flying buttress, south choir clerestory (see **31**). (B): Reconstructed elevation of the upper part of the triple scallop capital re-used in 14th century on the north side of the choir clerestory (**29**). This is a massive stone *c.*117cm deep. The area within the dashed lines shows the surviving face of the stone with the carved details. (C): Profile of double half-round shafts on the respond at the chord of the apse in the chapter house.
A and B could be part of the late 11th century choir vaulting arch and respond on the chord of the apse.

Groin vault and clerestory windows
Wilson proposed that a groin vault in the choir would allow room for windows accessed by the high-level passages in the transepts; he suggested that such passages were open to the choir

31 Two views of paired soffit rolls re-used under a buttress on the south side of the 14th-century choir.

via triple arches, with two of the monolithic columns (described above) in each opening (Wilson 1985, 53 fig2). Wilson proposed small clerestory windows within the external blind arcading (Wilson 1980, 128-9) (**32**A & B, **33, 34**) but later suggested larger ones (Wilson 1985, 53, 71) (**32**C). It has been argued that the larger window interrupts too much the rhythm of the blind arcading (Thurlby 1985a, 45; McAleer 1986, 171).

Barrel vault without clerestory windows
Exterior blind arcading in comparable buildings is frequently accompanied by a barrel vault

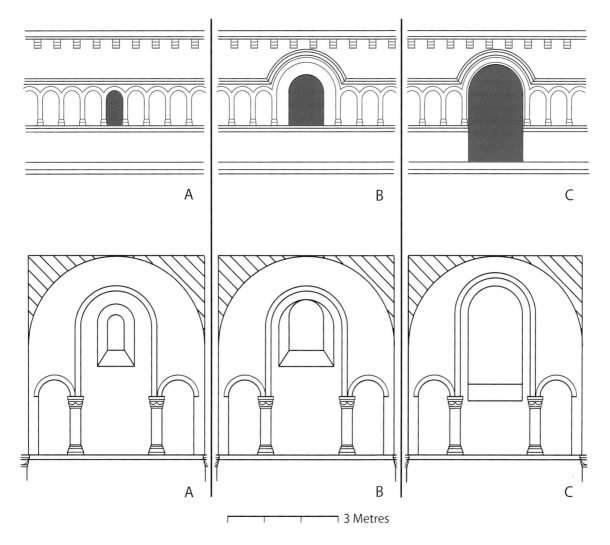

A   B   C

⌐   ⌐   ⌐   3 Metres

32 Choir, north side: external and internal elevations showing alternative reconstructions of clerestory windows (A) occupying one bay of the blind arcade (B) occupying three bays of the blind arcade, (C) occupying three bays of the blind arcade and extending down to the string course above the ambulatory roof (cf Wilson 1985, 53).

(Thurlby 1985b, 9-10); this would leave no room for clerestory windows (Thurlby 1985a, 45; McAleer 1986, 170; Fernie 2000, 157) (**35**).[18] There could however as McAleer suggests have been a high-level passage with openings only into the interior, as in the transepts of Tewkesbury and Pershore (McAleer 1986, 168) (**37**, **38**);

18 Our reconstruction (**35**) orginally used the photogrammetry of the south ambulatory, checked as correct when the survey of the north ambulatory became available in 2018.

these could have had paired openings with one of the monolithic columns at the centre of each pair, like those at Tewkesbury (Thurlby 2003, 100, figs 9.23 and 9.24).

A barrel vault, though very dark, would be in keeping with the severe style of Serlo's east end. In mitigation, Thurlby (*pers comm*) suggests the three bays of the apse could have been devoid of external blind arcading and instead have carried three large clerestory windows about 1.5m high lighting the east end.

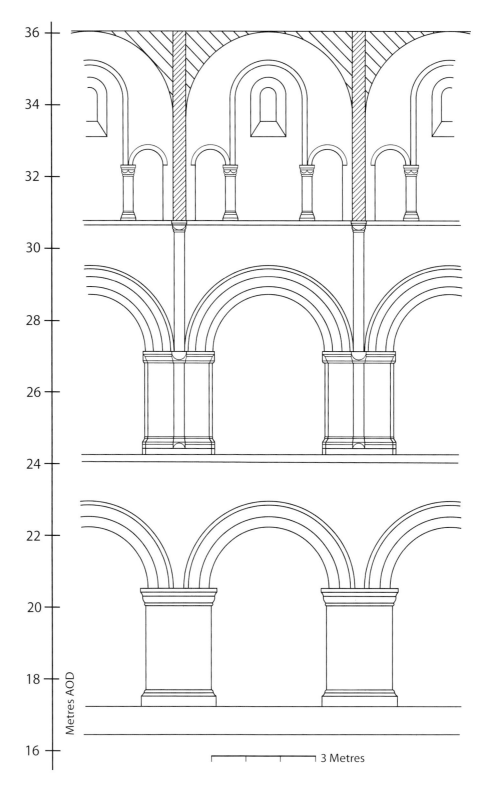

Metres AOD

3 Metres

33 Choir: reconstructed elevation of the north side, with groin-vault; clerestory windows are set into the exterior blind arcading (see **32** and **34**). Based on Wilson 1985, fig2, adjusted as to levels and with other modifications.

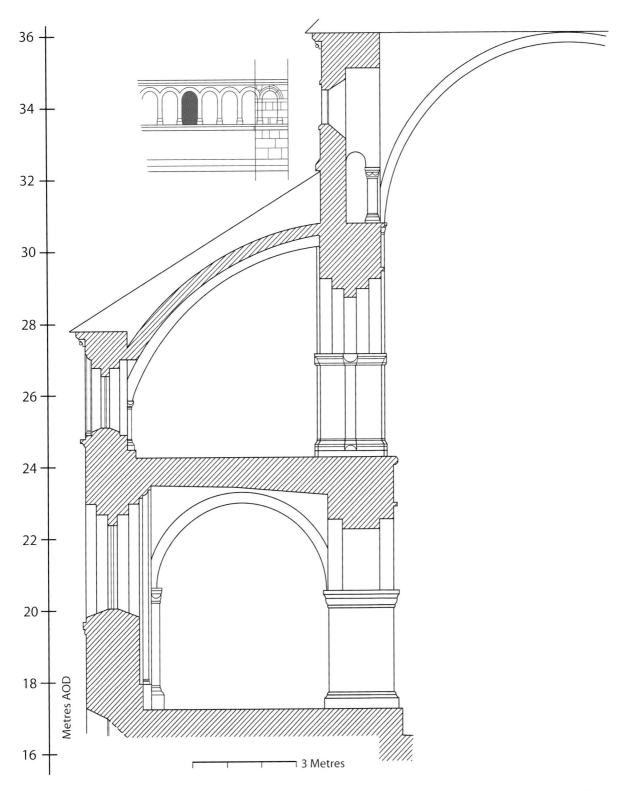

36 —

34 —

32 —

30 —

28 —

26 —

24 —

22 —

20 —

18 —

Metres AOD

16 —

3 Metres

34 Choir: reconstructed cross-section of the northern half with groin-vault and small clerestory windows, one of which is shown in dark tone in an external elevation. Based on Wilson 1985, fig3, adjusted as to levels and with other modifications.

The eastern chapels

The south-east and north-east radiating chapels that open from the eastern apse are the same in plan over the three storeys of crypt, choir ambulatory and tribune gallery. The eastern 'axial' chapel was similar but it only survives in the crypt and was recorded in 2017 as foundations at choir level. Each of the chapels consists of a rectangular bay with a polygonal apse (in the crypt the inner faces of the apses are half-round). The crypt chapels and the surviving ambulatory chapels are groin vaulted. The rectangular bays in the tribune gallery chapels are barrel vaulted with groin vaulting over the apses. The vault arches spring from engaged half-round shafts with cushion or scallop capitals and simple round bases. The walls of the choir

35 Choir: reconstructed north external elevation of three bays of the ambulatory and tribune gallery, with blind arcading on the high-level choir elevation.

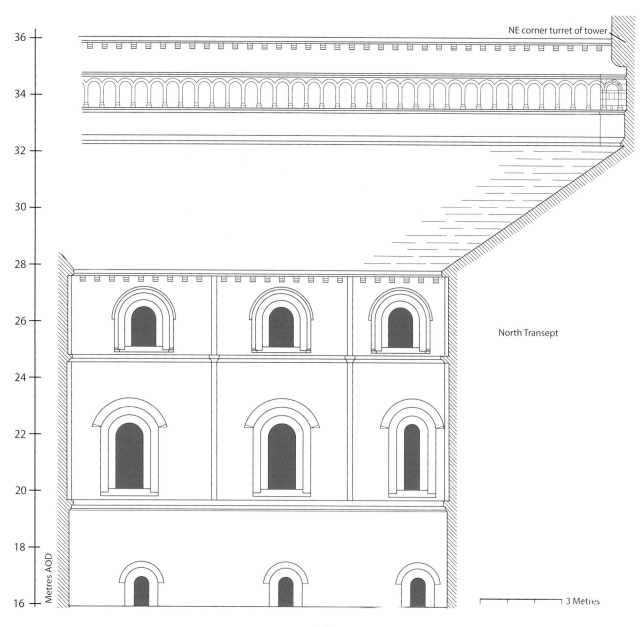

NE corner turret of tower

North Transept

Metres AOD

3 Metres

26

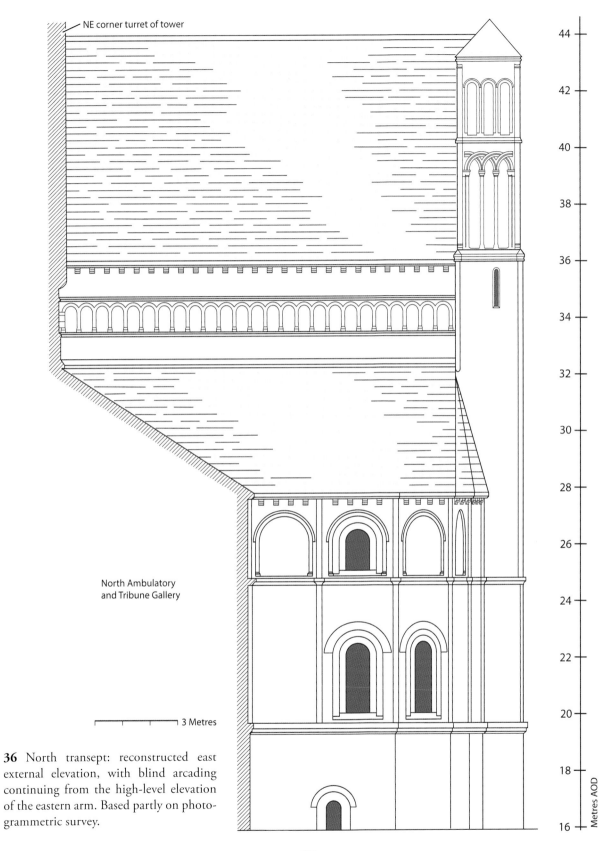

NE corner turret of tower

North Ambulatory
and Tribune Gallery

3 Metres

36 North transept: reconstructed east external elevation, with blind arcading continuing from the high-level elevation of the eastern arm. Based partly on photogrammetric survey.

44

42

40

38

36

34

32

30

28

26

24

22

20

18

16

Metres AOD

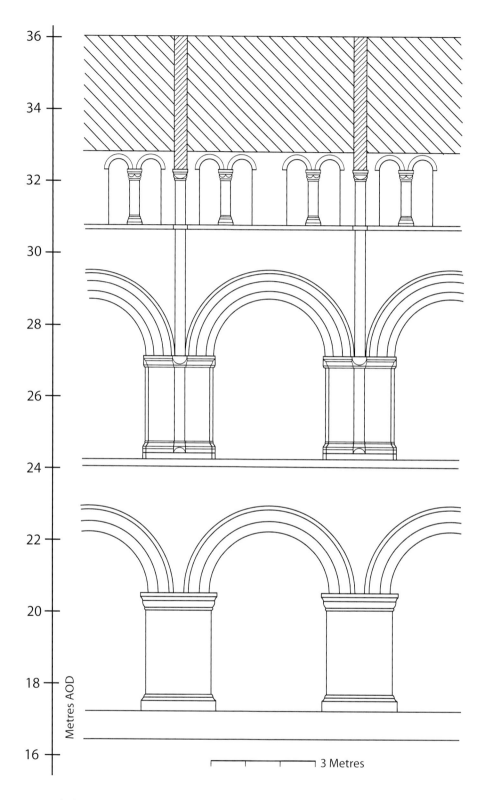

37 Choir: interior north elevation, reconstruction with segmental barrel-vault and high-level passage with openings to the interior. Partly based on Wilson 1985, fig2, modified.

28

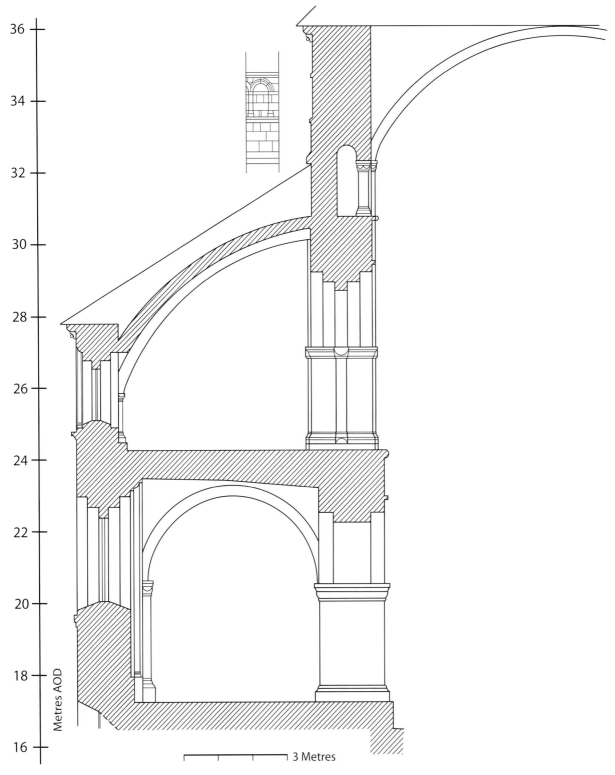

38 Choir: reconstructed cross-section of the northern side, with segmental barrel-vault, high-level passage and no windows at clerestory level. An external elevation of the surviving blind arcading is shown. Partly based on Wilson 1985, fig3: modified.

ambulatory chapels are recessed and outlined with continuous quadrant mouldings. The mouldings rise from raised sills that might have acted as benches. Excavations in the south-east chapel in 1992 (Heighway 1993) found the sill or bench in the central panel of the apse buried below the later reredos. The opposing chapel on the north-east was identical in other respects and presumably also had raised sills or benches. Observation in the Lady Chapel for Project Pilgrim in 2017 established that the original eastern axial chapel had sills or benches on the north and south sides, but it was not possible to establish if these continued around the inner face of the apse because this area could not be excavated. The corresponding chapels in the tribune gallery have side sills or benches only.

39 View to the south-east of the outside of the north-east tribune chapel showing the blind arcading on two faces. There was a single window in the central bay at tribune level, later replaced by the 14th-century window. A and B: original Romanesque windows with 'wedge springers' (inset). C: 14th-century window punched through a formerly blank wall. D: Romanesque window enlarged with voussoirs and wedge springers surviving on either side.

Windows and nook shafts

A few of the windows in the eastern arm of Serlo's original build survive unaltered as well as the double-splayed windows in the crypt.

At least three of the windows of the choir-level ambulatory appear to be late 11th century: this is confirmed by examination of the tooling and mortars. They are of unusual form, with segmental arches, enabling the jambs to rise higher than would be possible with a full semi-circular head. Instead of conventional springers the arches rise from small 'wedge' springers.[19] Internally the arches were semi-circular, with the continuous roll around each. Originally all the windows in the eastern arm at ambulatory level were of this type (as Steve Bagshaw observed - see **23**), though many were altered in the 14th century or subsequently.[20] For instance, the first window west of the north-east chapel (**39**D) has had the jambs cut back, the arch raised and the sill lowered. Part of the original voussoirs with their 'wedge' springers survive on either side.

The blind arches at tribune level in the various chapels, were also altered in the later medieval period: one (**40**) received new (or adapted?) moulded voussoirs (B) and inserted capitals (C, D), one polygonal.

It is uncertain whether Serlo's build had nook-shafts. The early 12th-century inner elevations of the nave north aisle windows (see below pp63-4) have nook shafts with scalloped capitals (**82**A).

In the straight tribune bays any Romanesque

40 Blind arch at the junction of the eastern arm and the north transept. The shaft and base (**40**A) is a retained portion of the original continuous soffit roll.

19 Windows were pierced in the 14th/15th century in the blank walls of the ambulatory chapels (**39**). The evidence was noted and recorded by Pascal Mychalysin and his team: we are grateful to them for allowing us to visit in 2019 and for their explanations. Pascal also noted that the mortar and style of the ball-flower window in the tribune north-east chapel matches that of the south aisle windows, dated to 1316.

20 Some mouldings from the continuous rolls of the 11th-century windows are re-used in two of the south choir roof-space windows: the window-head was created in the 14th century to concord with the Romanesque mouldings. See GCAR 93/H, where the mouldings are wrongly described as nook-shafts.

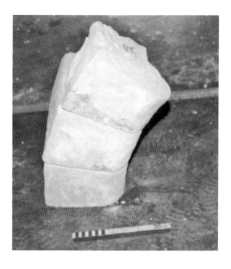
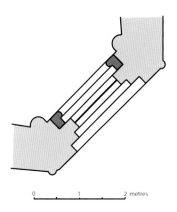

41 Voussoirs with a soffit roll (the outer edge of which was flush with the wall face) found built into the 14th-century reredos of the south-east chapel. They probably came from the inner face of the original chapel window as shown in darker shading in the reconstructed plan.

windows have been entirely replaced in the 14th century by round-headed windows with wave mouldings (**42**). Bagshaw (2000, 4) thought that there were originally no windows at all at tribune gallery level and it is true that unlike the ambulatory level below there are no voussoirs or other remnants. However we find it hard to believe that the tribune gallery ambulatories would not have been lit. We have therefore reconstructed the gallery windows the same size

42 Tribune gallery, south side. 14th century round-headed windows, each with a wave moulding carved as an outer frame on the arris between the wall face and the soffit.

as the surviving blind arches around the eastern chapels, with the continuous roll moulding on the exterior.

It is possible that, in keeping with the widespread use of continuous rolls around the arches of the early phase of Serlo's building, the window surrounds in the interior elevations of the east end were also decorated with continuous rolls rather than the nook-shafts that are used in the north aisle of the nave. This suggestion received support from the excavation of the reredos in the south-east ambulatory chapel in 1992 (Heighway 1993) which discovered seven sections of jambs and voussoirs with a soffit roll 15.3cm wide. The outer edge of the soffit roll was flush with the wall face (41). The jambs and voussoirs came from an opening 1.4m wide and are probably from the inner face of one of the original chapel windows. They carried whitewash and fictive ashlars in red paint.

There are however nook-shafts in the 11th-century north-east gallery chapel. The sill of the window in the central bay of the chapel was lowered in the 14th century and its head was raised and decorated with ballflower. Its jambs carry nook-shafts with plain bases and cushion capitals. The shafts extend up into the raised 14th-century fabric. They have therefore been extended upwards and downwards (43), but they could nevertheless have originated here. There are no longer nook-shafts in the south-east chapel at the same level: these could have been the source for the extended shafts in the north-east chapel.

There are re-used nook-shafts on the 14th-century south choir clerestory elevation where they total at least 35m of shaft and nine scalloped capitals (44, 45). These may have come from the nave south aisle, rebuilt a decade earlier: this would have made available 84m of shafts (internal and external), 28 bases, and at least 14 capitals: however, can we accept that these would be kept in storage for so long? A more likely

source for these shafts would be from the south elevation of the south transept. This is discussed in more detail below (pp43-5).

43 Interior of north-east tribune chapel showing re-set nook shaft. *WD*

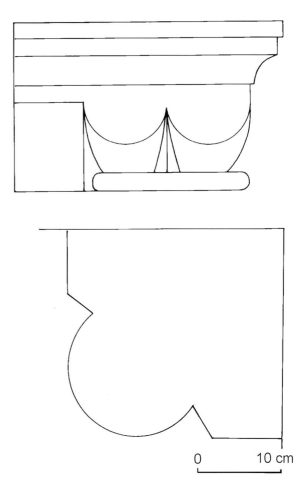

45 South side of the choir clerestory, third window from the west. Elevation of capital; profile of shaft.
Drawings: R Bossons

44 Nook shafts and capitals re-used on the 14th-century windows of the south elevation of the choir clerestory.

THE TRANSEPTS AND TOWER

The south transept (**46**) was transformed in the 1330s (Wilson 1980, 113-134; Welander 1991, 150-160); the north transept (**47**) was similarly altered 1368-74 after the refurbishment of the choir (Welander 1991, 216-19). The 14th-century alterations involved the refacing of all

46 The east side of the south transept, refaced with 14th-century mouldings, panelling and tracery. *AH*.

47 The east side of north transept, refaced with 14th-century mouldings, panelling and tracery. *AH.*

the elevations in new masonry, new vaulting and the insertion of large windows in both north and south elevations. On the east elevations, the Romanesque galleries and chapels were retained. The lowest 10m of the walls of the west and south external elevations were originally plain[1] (Bagshaw 2002b fig3). Each transept consisted of two unequal bays: the inner bay the width of the choir ambulatories and nave aisles, the outer bay somewhat wider with an eastern chapel.

Each transept had a stair-turret in the outer western corner — there were no passages or galleries on the west side of the transepts and

there was no connection between any of the transept passages and the nave clerestory passage. The transept stair turrets gave access to eastward-leading passages in the thickness of the walls at two levels; one at choir tribune level (24.2m AOD), and one higher (30.7m AOD). The north-east corner of the north transept and the south-east corner of the south transept also contained stairs but only above clerestory level and in the thickness of the walls: these stairs gave access to the roof leads (Wilson 1985, 72, fig10)[2].

These passages were all obliterated in the 14th century by the insertion of windows. However,

---

1 The south face of the south transept has a door (known now as the Pilgrims' Door) and a small round-headed window: these are later insertions. The north transept exterior had the arcades and vault of the monks' parlour (**99**) built against it.

2 The 14th-century adaptations mean that access to the north-east and south-east high level passages is via the stair in the north-west and south-west turrets, up to the roof level, and down the corresponding stair in the opposing turrets.

access to the Romanesque choir tribune gallery was maintained by lowering the gallery-level passages to the base of the new north and south windows.[3]

The transeptal turrets

The top two stages of the corner turrets of the transepts are decorated with overlap arcading and blind arches (**57, 58**). These may have been added in the 12th century (Wilson 1980, 128) — Bagshaw (2002b, 3-4) recorded evidence that the top stages of the turrets, initially timber, were replaced after a fire. In addition some of the turret arcading incorporates re-used recut chevron voussoirs (*ibid*, 7, fig16). Originally the string course dividing the upper parts of the turrets consisted of a course of green sandstone (*ibid*, 6, fig12).

The north transept

The best information about the Romanesque appearance derives from the north transept, which retains much of its original form behind the 14th-century casing (**47, 48**). On the ground floor the outer order of the chapel entrance has a surrounding soffit roll without capitals, in the

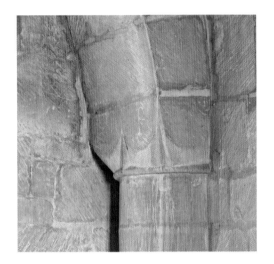

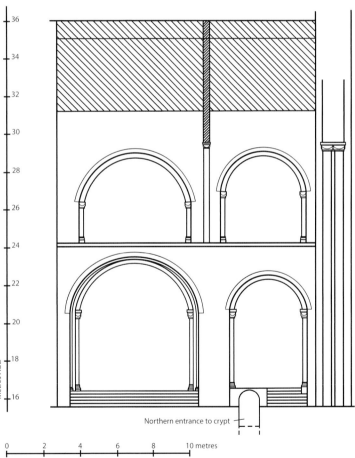

48 East elevation of north transept reconstructed from remains visible behind 14th-century façade. Inset above: springer voussoir carved as scallop capital in the tribune gallery. *MT.*

Northern entrance to crypt

0   2   4   6   8   10 metres

3 The passage below the south transept south window has blind alcoves on its inner south face which seem however to be related to 14th-century or

later structures and not a remnant of the Romanesque fenestration.

37

severe Serlo style. Within that is another order with double half-shafts supporting cushion capitals and a plain arch. The chapel itself is groin-vaulted with windows and blind arches, all these are surrounded by a continuous roll without capitals. At tribune level, the inner order arches of both bays have unusual springer voussoirs carved as scallop capitals (**48 inset**).[4]

The high-level passage at clerestory level is accessed in an unusual way. The entrance to the passage from the north-west turret is at only 27m AOD, 3m lower than its south transept equivalent.

49 North transept, entrance to clerestory passage, east end, showing downward westward slope of passage vault.

4 These did not appear in the corresponding position on the south side.

However the door level is misleading.[5] The other end of the passage is visible inside the north-east turret[6] where it was 3m higher, and where the blocked passage entrance leading west can be seen, with its vault sloping down (**49**). Another passage at the same level leads south onto what is now the sill of the eastern transept clerestory window.[6] Thus the passage in the north transept north wall rises from 27m AOD in the north-west tower to 30m AOD in the north-east tower. The 3m rise in height could have been accomplished either by one flight of steps in the east quarter of the transept north wall, or by having half the flight at the western end (as **50**).

There is no obvious reason why the arrangements of passageways in the north transept was not a mirror image of the south where the passage ran horizontally (below p44).

On the west side of the transept can still be seen the vestiges of the originally-intended quadrant vault of the nave aisle (Wilson 1985, 73). One voussoir (**51**) is still *in situ*.

The decoration of the north transept gable

The gable end of the north transept, like that of the south transept, was probably re-used from the Romanesque gable (Heighway 2007b; Mychalysin 2007), and may originally have been installed before 1100. It has unique 'T' mouldings reminiscent of chopped-off beak-head (**52**).[7]

5 Thurlby assumed that the clerestory-level passage was all at this level, and that it was therefore too low to be associated with a choir clerestory: Thurlby 1985a, 46. McAleer (1986, 169) noticed the discrepancy in levels, but offered no explanation.

6 The floor in the turret is at 30m AOD, steps up 70cm to the south, and descends in the window well to 30.37m AOD. Here as in the corresponding position in the south transept, the well of the window was probably in the 14th century cut down into the passage base, and the original level of the passage was about 30.7m AOD, as it would need to be to clear the tribune vaults.

7 We have been unable to find parallels for the T-mouldings. The north transept face otherwise shows no sign of any former decoration: it is entirely taken up with the 14th-century window and was totally obscured by the building of the library and room below in the late 14th century.

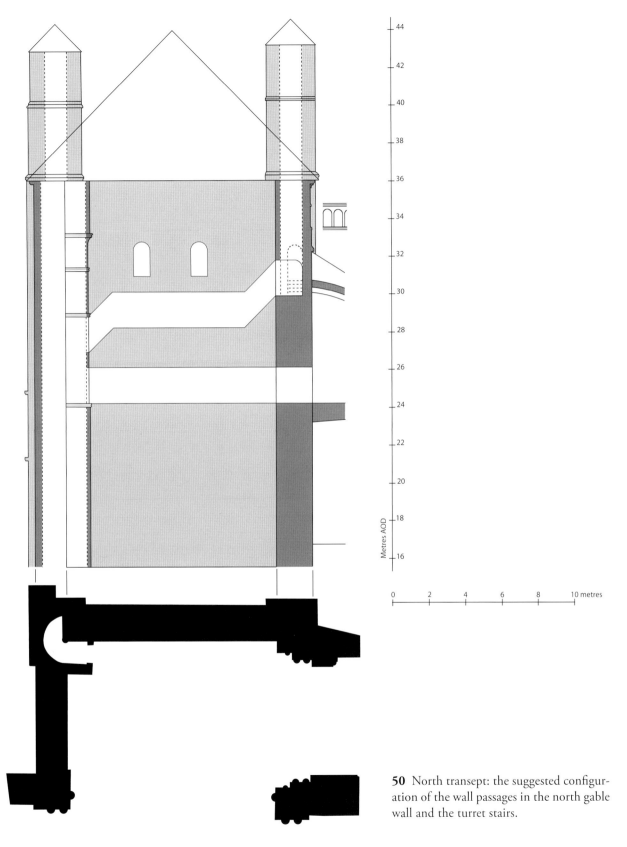

50 North transept: the suggested configuration of the wall passages in the north gable wall and the turret stairs.

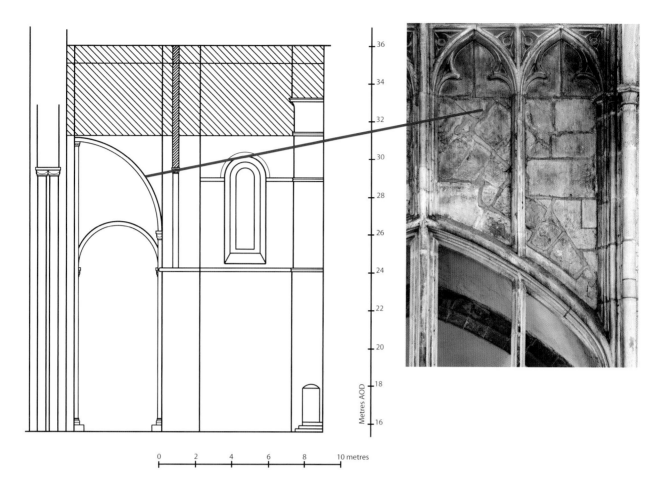

51 Left: North transept: reconstructed west elevation, following Wilson 1985, 73; illustrated in Welander 1991, 49. Right: The remains of the high quadrant arch in the west wall of the north transept. One voussoir is still *in situ* behind 14th-century facade mouldings and, to the right, the curve of the arch shows in the upper edge of the later infill. *WD*

The transept vaults

The transepts were probably vaulted.[8] The width to be spanned was, after all, about the same as that spanned in the choir, where there is some evidence for a groin or barrel vault (above p14). The presence of external arcading might also be an indication of a barrel vault (Thurlby 1985b, 9-10). On both internal stair turrets there are string-courses. The lowest in each case marks gallery level

(24.2m AOD). The next one at 29.2m may relate to the position of lost windows, whilst the string course at 31.4m[9] is probably the height from which the vault springs. Just below 33m AOD, the turrets become wider (**53, 54, 55, 56**). This widening of the turret plan, now well below the 14th-century vault, was surely above the original vault, and was not intended to be visible. The widening was disguised in the 14th century with an outward-flaring profile below a string course.

8 Wilson assumed, because the string courses on the turrets showed no sign of disturbance by barrel vaults, that there was originally a wooden ceiling (Wilson 1985, 72). There is in fact room above the highest string course for a segmental barrel vault. According to Wilson only the string courses on the north transept turret are 12th century.

9 all +/- 10cm, due to having to measure from the floor with a digital instrument to the underside of the mouldings.

52 North transept north gable, showing the distinctive 'T'-mouldings around the blind arcading. *Photo: RD.*
Inset: mason's template drawing of the 'T'-moulding.

Our reconstruction of the vault (**56**) has been dictated by the necessity of ensuring that the vault is below the widening of the turret already described. A groin vault would have exposed the turret widening; only a barrel vault can be positioned so as to hide the wider section of the turret. We therefore reconstruct the transept with a barrel vault (the same argument applies to the south transept). This interpretation requires the vault to be set too low to allow high-level windows or even interior openings from the eastern high-level passages.

There would therefore have been little light from the east side of the transepts other than the limited amount from the chapel windows and from the gallery windows. We suggest that there were two lights in the north elevation of the north transept, which would of necessity have been set high enough to avoid the position of the wall passages.[10] We also suggest a single light in the west elevation.

10 Similar fenestration could have operated in the south transept, except that because of the different position of the wall passages, the two lights in the south wall would have to be set lower.

41

53, 54 North transept north-west turret showing string courses and stepping-out of turret masked by a flaring moulding below the 14th-century vaulting.

55 South transept south-west turret, showing string courses and stepping-out of turret masked by a flaring moulding below the 14th-century vaulting.

42

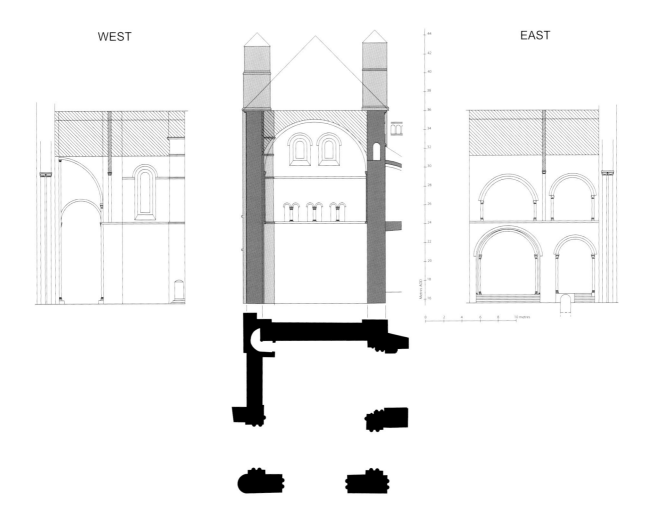

WEST   EAST

56 North transept: plan and reconstructed elevations with a barrel vault. The vault is set at a height to obscure the step-out in the plan of the north-west turret, which must have been above the original vault. The soffit face of the transverse arch has been projected onto the elevation from the south and is of a slightly smaller diameter because it springs from a thickening of the wall at the junction of the west wall of the transept and the north wall of the north aisle (see plan). The windows in the north elevation are assumed, as is the window in the western elevation The tribune-level wall passage is shown lit from a series of paired openings with monolithic shafts in each one. The eastern elevation is reconstructed from remains still visible. The barrel vault does not allow for clerestory level windows or passage windows.

The south transept

(**57**) In the 14th century most of the south elevation between the turrets was taken out and rebuilt more than a metre further north on what had been the inside face of the Romanesque south wall (**58**). The gable was re-set further back still (it rests in fact on the 14th-century vaulting rather than on any part of the south wall).

The rebuilding necessitated the elimination of the wall-passages. The lower passage was lowered to below the 14th-century south window; the entrance to the higher passage was converted into a window (**59**), through which can be seen the corresponding opening on the south-east turret at the same level (**60**). Both openings are at 30m AOD. In the south-east turret, the doorway which

57 The external south face of the south transept. *AH.*

gave access to the passage in the eastern wall now opens onto the sill of the south transept east clerestory window, also at 30m AOD. It is clear that the passage led horizontally from the south-west to the south-east stair-turret and from there turned north towards the crossing.

The whole of the external 14th-century elevation is decorated with re-used Romanesque material: chevron, nook shafts, and scalloped capitals. A window 11.5m high at the apex carries lateral-to-face chevron; the jambs have nook shafts topped with scalloped capitals. Above the window to east and west are blind pointed arches of frontal-face chevron supported on scalloped capitals and nook shafts. The outer edges of the former south wall, now acting as buttresses, carries vertical

strings of frontal-face chevron, 9.3m high on each side.

Re-used on the east and west elevations are more nook shafts and scallop capitals, as well as a pair of beast-head label stops (**61**).[11]

There is plentiful evidence that this was re-use for deliberate architectural effect, and that sometimes the 14th-century masons ran out of suitable decorated stone and had to make more in the original Romanesque style.[12]

The source of all this ornament was presumably the south transept itself. If this is correct and if it was complete by 1100 it would have been a startling departure from the style of the rest of Serlo's east end, which used a 'severity of design that excluded not only carved decoration but such conventional niceties as abaci' (Wilson 1980, 128-29). It would also represent an early use of chevron ornament (p101).

The interior of the south transept has been the subject of much comment by architectural historians (Massé 1898, 65; Wilson 1980, 139-40; Morris 2003). It was refurbished after the burial in the abbey presbytery of king Edward II, and was reputedly funded by the many visitors to his tomb, though plentiful royal donations must have been involved (Luxford 2005, 158). Wilson explained the fact that work started in the south transept rather than in the choir by suggesting that the work was an initial trial for future work; we wonder if an additional reason was that serious remedial work was needed. Severe movement is very evident. The arches in the east face of the transept, except that into the choir aisle, have been reinforced by the insertion of much narrower

11 West side north window:- south jamb, capital used as a base (Bagshaw 2002b, fig19); east clerestory window:- nook shafts, frontal-face chevron, and beast-head label stop (Heighway 1999). The southern beast-head is a Victorian replacement.
12 Ashwell 1985. The same was true of the north transept. Close examination of the north transept gable showed mismatch of voussoirs, evidence that the gable decoration was re-assembled from dismantled pieces; also some of the '12th century' decoration was actually remade from 12th-century roll-mouldings turned round (Heighway 2007b, 2-3).

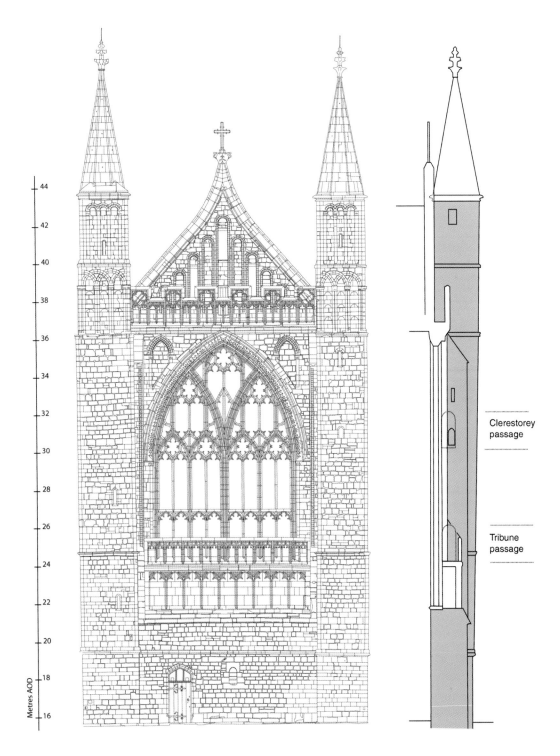

Clerestorey passage

Tribune passage

Metres AOD

58 South transept: exterior photogrammetric elevation. The cross section, with the south-east turret in elevation, shows how the wall between the turrets was entirely taken down in the 14th century and set back about a metre.

45

59 South transept south-west turret, entrance doorway to clerestory passage, view to east, blocked and converted into a window.

60 South transept south-west turret: view through window in former clerestory passage (**59**), looking at corresponding doorway in the south-east turret.

pointed arches (**62, 63**), and the southern two of these carry quadrant mouldings. These have been cleverly integrated into the 14th-century work but it is clear that they were originally meant to show. In the tribune gallery it can be seen that the other side of this arch is decorated with a roll above scallop capitals surmounting nook shafts (**64**). In the outer order of the original Romanesque arch several voussoirs have buckled downwards (**65**). Above this arch there is a crack presumably resulting from the continuing movement of the south-east turret, which today as has already been remarked (p10, n6) leans out by about 40cm at the top.

The northern tribune arch has also been filled

with a narrower pointed arch of a rather different design to the two in the southern bay. The inner order of the Romanesque original of this arch had actually fallen out (or had to be removed) before the blocking arch was inserted (**66**). This pointed arch seems to be of a date with one of the diagonal buttresses (Bagshaw 2002b, 10) which

61 South transept, east elevation of clerestory. The fragment of possible Romanesque string-course (see n15 p19) is indicated.

were inserted in the 14th century in the east and west walls of the transept to support the tower.[13]

Since some of this movement was already occuring in the 12th century, it is possible that it affected the south front sufficently to occasion refurbishing (cf. Wilson 1985, 72). The crypt had already needed to be reinforced (above p9).

We have speculatively reconstructed a Roman-esque external elevation (**67**) derived from re-used elements of the 14th-century one. We premise a design dominated by a blind arch decorated with chevron,[14] enclosing a pair of single-light windows. The arch and the windows have jambs with nook-shafts. Over the large chevron arch we suggest there was a roll-moulding as now to be seen on the east clerestory window of the south transept; below it we insert the beast-

13 The buttress on the west side of the transept is probably 14th-century work (Bagshaw 2002b, 17). That on the east, which now crosses the eastern chapel entrance, may also be this date, though F W Waller (1911, fig 10) supposed it to be 15th century. The lower part of this buttress was at some time further strengthened by a slightly narrower underpinning with a curving lower face. Finally the outer order on the east face of the chapel was infilled and decorated with Romanesque-style shafts and capitals. The capitals are different from those in the corresponding 11th-century examples in the north transept, being much deeper. So they may be re-used from elsewhere or else manufactured in the 14th century to imitate 11th century work. They have been mistaken in the past for 11th century work (as Wilson pointed out; 1980, 133 and n22). By the early 18th century the

chapel entrance was sealed off by a screen and a doorway had been created to the north into the choir ambulatory (Welander 1991, 404; Bonnor 1796); in the 19th century it was used as a vestry (Massé 1898, 67). By 1855 the chapel entrance was blocked by monuments, and Waller recommended opening it up (Heighway 2007b, 213): this may have been the occasion when the buttress which crossed the entrance to the chapel was restored– much of the tooling and appearance of the present buttress is Victorian.

14 Ashwell (1985, 115) reached the same conclusion: he calculated that a 14th-century chevron-decorated arch had been created from a semi-circular arch of radius 3.96m.

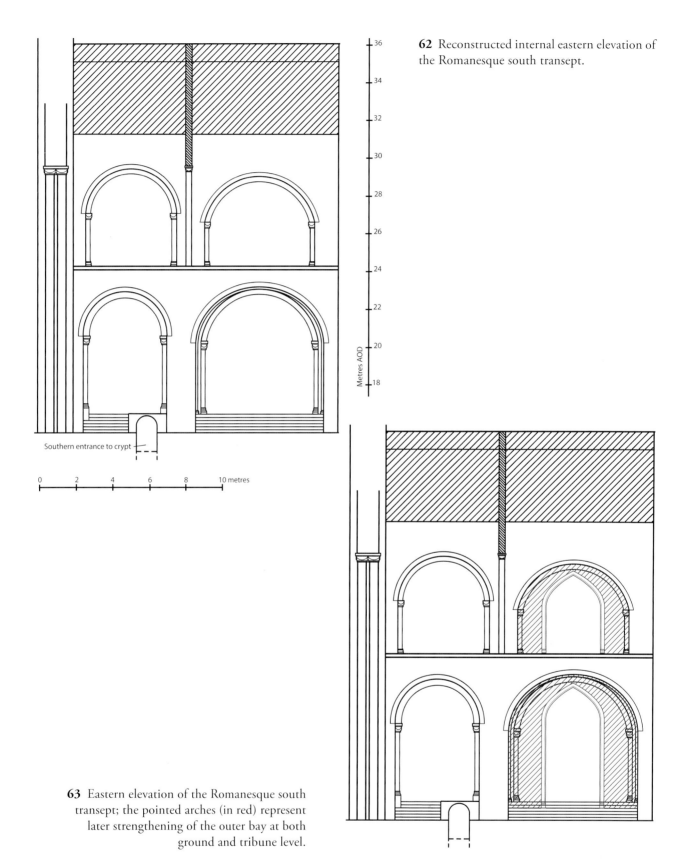

62 Reconstructed internal eastern elevation of the Romanesque south transept.

Metres AOD

Southern entrance to crypt

0   2   4   6   8   10 metres

63 Eastern elevation of the Romanesque south transept; the pointed arches (in red) represent later strengthening of the outer bay at both ground and tribune level.

64 Western arch of the south tribune chapel, showing the buckled voussoirs (arrowed) of the outer order of the Romanesque arch and the pointed reinforcing arch (looking south). *WD*

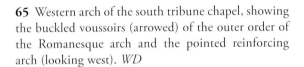

65 Western arch of the south tribune chapel, showing the buckled voussoirs (arrowed) of the outer order of the Romanesque arch and the pointed reinforcing arch (looking west). *WD*

66 The southern tribune gallery looking west, showing the reinforcing of the Romanesque arch with a pointed arch and a diagonal bracing buttress. *WD*

49

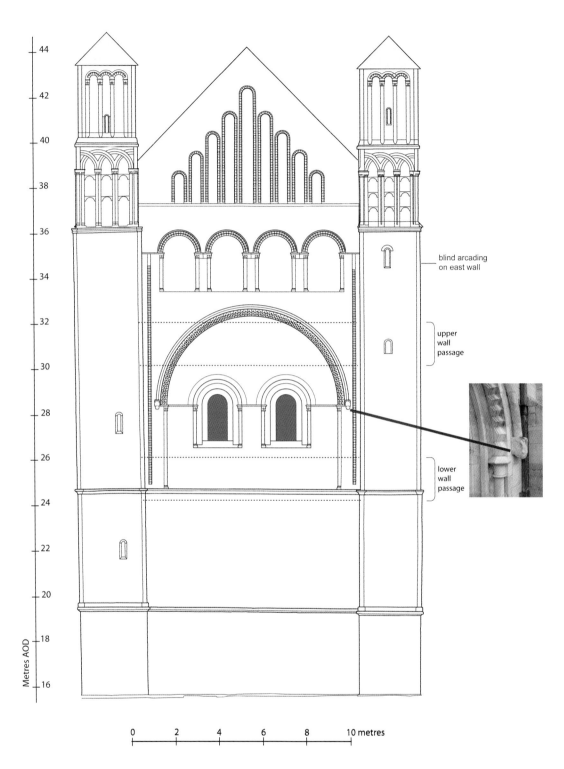

blind arcading
on east wall

upper
wall
passage

lower
wall
passage

Metres AOD

44

42

40

38

36

34

32

30

28

26

24

22

20

18

16

0   2   4   6   8   10 metres

67 South transept south elevation: a suggested reconstruction of the Romanesque design, incorporating material re-used in the 14th century. The pair of animal-head label-stops are reset on the east clerestory window of the south transept (inset). **58** shows the existing 14th-century elevation.

head label stops one of which can be seen in the same window. Above the arch we suggest a blind arcade of four round-headed arches decorated with chevron and nook shafts. It is possible that these blind arches could originally have been pointed as they are now, and that the elevation was composed of round and pointed arches in combination. (The springing of the main arch and of these blind arcade arches is unknown; we have derived it from the heights at which they were reused in the 14th century.) We also consider it highly likely that the gable decoration was re-set from the Romanesque gable.[15]

The Romanesque south transept elevation in our suggested reconstruction incorporates at least fourteen nook-shafts. The 14th-century re-use of all these would have provided a source for almost half of the nook-shafts of similar diameter on the south choir elevation, where the 14th-century clerestory windows make use of a total of 35m of shaft (diameter 16cm) as well as nine capitals and four bases (**44, 45**).

The tower

The only known feature of the Romanesque tower is that it had a cylindrical overhanging turret (**68**) at each corner. The remains of the western two of these are visible at the east end of the nave roof space (**69**), a third one survives externally (**26, 27**) showing that it extended 90cm below the 11th-century corbel table and terminated with an inverted 'dome'. The upper part of this turret is burnt red.[16] It survives up to about 40m AOD, above which it is rebuilt as a 14th or 15th century buttress.

The external diameter of the turrets was *c*.2.5m, so they are not large enough to contain a stair, and must have been simply decorative. Nevertheless, the south-east turret may have been larger than the other three and formed a stair access (in which case it would have to have extended lower on the tower).

These fragments of turrets are all that survive of a late 11th century tower. When choir and transepts were completed and roofed there must have been a tower at least at 43.5m AOD to support the adjacent roofs. Yet the tower interior viewed from just above the crossing vault (the space known as the 'star chamber') betrays no evidence of a Romanesque original (**70, 71**). The interior walls are built of ashlars of varying sizes: relatively small Romanesque blocks with diagonal tooling, and larger later medieval ones. All the walls contain occasional reddened blocks of stone, apparently inserted randomly, indicating re-use of earlier material; the same material including occasional reddened blocks was used for the vault relieving arches, which have every appearance of having been custom-built with a gap for the vault, the vault being inserted subsequently and the gap only very roughly filled with masonry. Whatever tower existed when the 14th-century choir was begun[17] was taken down entirely and rebuilt using recycled materials. This rebuild was used as a base in the 15th century when the present tower was constructed.

15 The present 14th-century gable slopes down to the inner face of the transept side-walls, and the 14th century roof (like other 14th-century and later roofs at the church) took rainwater into a stone gutter formed from the top of the side walls. The Romanesque roof, however, must have run straight from its apex to the outside of the outer wall, taking rainwater over the corbel-table (**67**).

16 Much of the early fabric of the abbey is scorch-marked deep red. There is no scorching on fabric of 14th-century date and it is assumed that reddened stone is an indication of late 11th/early 12th century work. The scorching could result from the fire of 1102 when the 'church together with the city was burnt' (Barber 1988, 603-4), or to 1122 when 'the city of Gloucester with the principal monastery' were burnt (ibid, 605) (the E text of the Anglo-Saxon Chronicle says the fire reached 'the upper part of the tower and all the monastery was burned and all the treasures that were there except a few books and three mass vestments': Whitelock, 188, s.a. 1122). Another fire in 1190 burned the city 'and almost all the workshops attached to the abbey' (Barber 1988, 611). Possibly these workshops were north of the abbey church, just east of the present boiler-house, where a large but localised patch of burning indicates buildings against the north ambulatory wall. The town was burnt again in 1214 and in 1223 (ibid, 612, 613) though on these occasions the fire might not have reached the abbey.

17 An 'eastern tower' was constructed in 1222 by Elias the Sacrist: Barber 1988, 613.

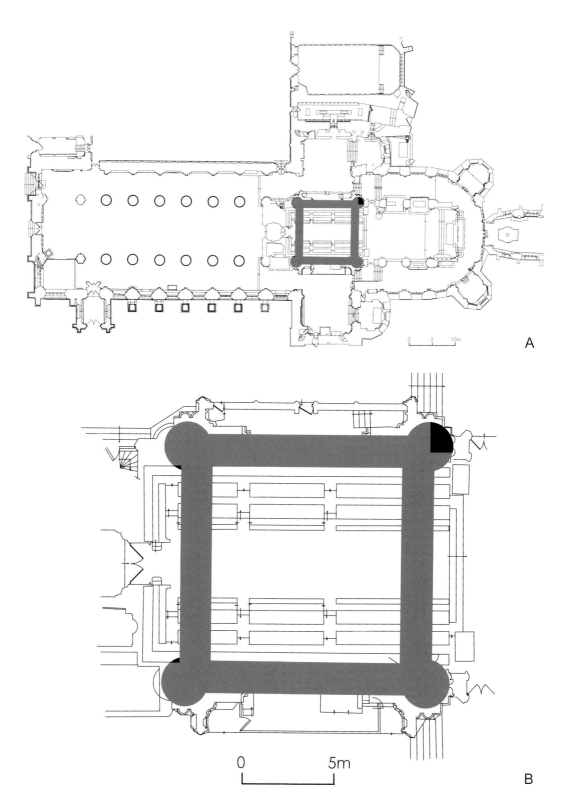

A

B

68 The Romanesque tower: A: reconstructed plan at roof-plate level superimposed on modern plan. B: enlarged detail to show surviving fragments (in black).

69 Nave roof space: east end looking north: remains of Romanesque corner turret.

70 Inside the medieval tower: the 'star chamber' just above the 14th century vault. View of west wall.

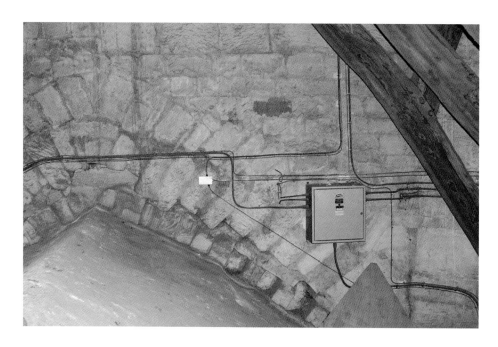

71 Inside the medieval tower, view of east wall. All the masonry used for the arches over the vault seems similar to the wall in which it is placed: occasional reddened blocks occur in both locations.

THE NAVE

The early 12th-century Romanesque nave survives almost in its entirety (**72**). The elevation of the clerestory has been reconstructed by Wilson (Welander 1991, 66, derived from Wilson 1980). A high vault of some sort is suggested by the extensive disturbance behind and beside the 13th-century vault shafts, indicating something replaced (**4**, **79**), probably a quadripartite rib vault over single bays (Thurlby 1985a, 47-8).

The giant columns — presently 8.6m high from

72 Romanesque nave from the west. *AH*

73 Eastern piers of the nave: octagonal plinth.

floor to the bottom of the capitals — would have been even higher in their original form, since the floor has been raised by up to 10 cm. over the centuries. Only one Romanesque square base plinth for the columns has been recorded, on the second southern pier from the west end; the top of the plinth was at 14.7 AOD and the floor that related to it would have been even lower. In the 17th century octagonal bases were added around the columns, and these in turn were replaced in 1856 with the present torus mouldings set on square plinths (Heighway 2003, 34). The easternmost pair of columns still have octagonal bases, set at a higher level beside the choir screen (**73**): if these are the original Romanesque arrangement they represent different treatment of the significant east end (Thurlby 2012, 43). The capitals are very similar to those in the eastern arm of the church. The arcade arches have plain soffits but the nave face of each is decorated with face-out chevron and edged with a chamfered hood moulding with square stops (**76**). The arch of the last 12th century bay in the north arcade, at the west end of the nave, is rather more richly decorated with a small, large-eyed animal mask

(**116**C) at the centre of the billet-decorated hood moulding.

Gloucester nave had no gallery to match that in the choir but instead had a triforium less than 3m high and without a passage (**77**). The triforium openings are accessed from the aisle roof spaces, originally via a large arch, now through a small door in the arch blocking. The openings consist of pairs of chevron-decorated arches each of which encloses a further pair of arches. The shafts of the arches are round, with scallop capitals and simple round bases.

The plan at triforium level (**79**) shows that the chevron-ornamented string course represented a substantial 'shelf' at the base of the triforium. This 'shelf', it has been suggested, originally supported the responds of a 12th-century nave vault (Wilson 1980, 379, n20; Thurlby 1985a, 48). We have reconstructed triple vault-shafts (following Wilson) in approximately the same position as the 13th-century ones, but the shafts are set side-by-side so that they require more 'width' and less 'depth' and they are fully seated on the 'shelf'.

We assume that the chevron-decorated semicircular 'platforms' from which spring the present

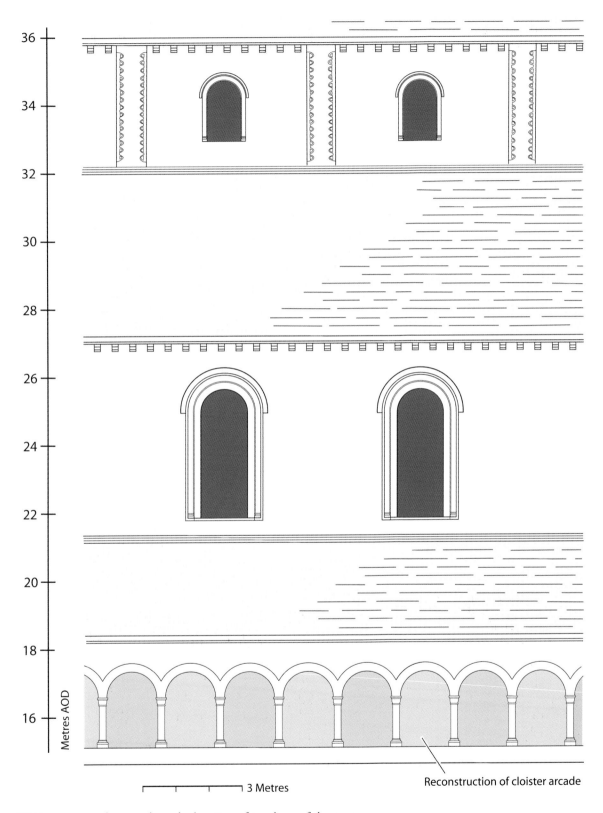

74 Reconstructed external north elevation of two bays of the nave.

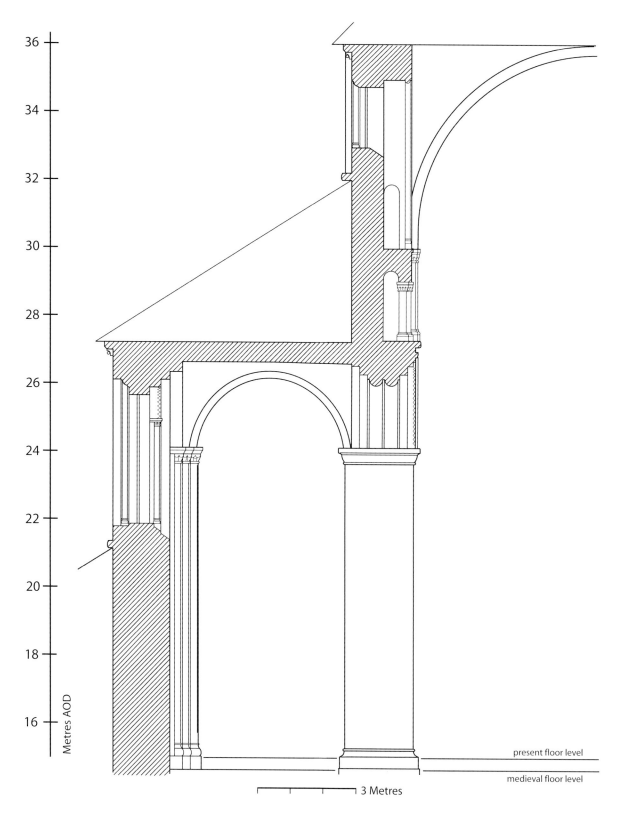

36 —

34 —

32 —

30 —

28 —

26 —

24 —

22 —

20 —

Metres AOD

18 —

16 —

present floor level

medieval floor level

3 Metres

75 Reconstructed cross-section of the nave and north aisle.

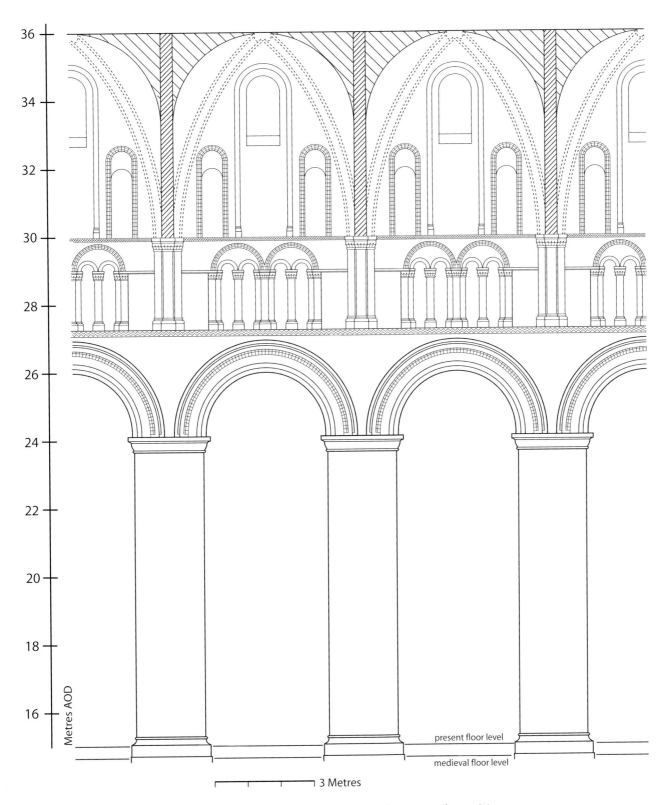

Metres AOD

present floor level

medieval floor level

3 Metres

76 Nave, reconstruction of the internal south elevation (caption details continued on p60).

77 Nave, triforium from the west. *Photograph: Skycell*

---

76 (continued) The great arcade columns are significantly higher than previous records have suggested. This is partly the result of a series of new measurements taken, by the authors, on the columns and on the soffit-faces of each of the orders of the arcade arches, and partly due to reinstating the lower part of the columns, now hidden below raised floor-levels but recorded during archaeological observations. The present bases are false. The diagonal vaulting ribs have been shown as dotted lines so that the full face of the elevation can be seen. We have assumed that the Romanesque vaulting ribs rose from flattish, grouped shafts that sat on uninterrupted string courses at tribune level (see **79**). The projecting chevron-decorated upper parts of the supports for the 13th-century vaulting shafts are later alterations to the original design. Based on Wilson as published in Welander 1991, 66. Detail added, levels and height of columns adjusted.

78 13th-century vaulting shafts with vertical scars on either side presumably from the removal of Romanesque fabric.

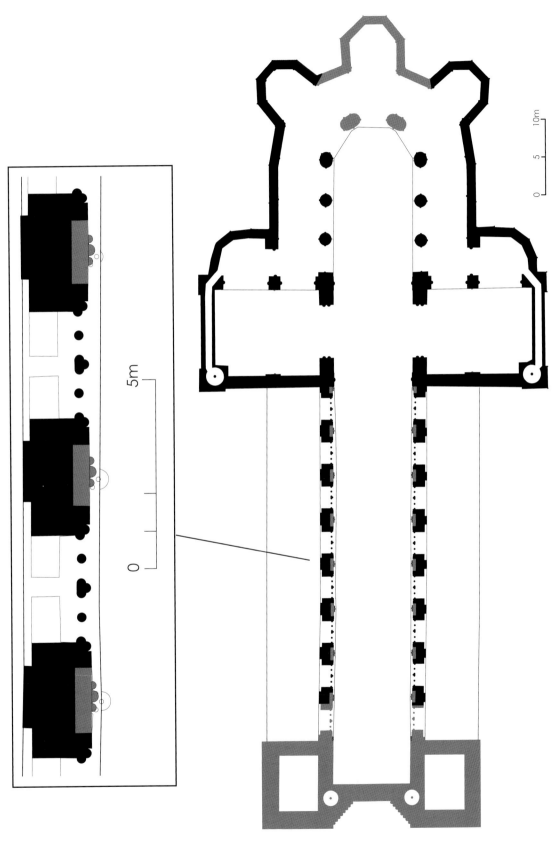

79 The tribune/triforium plan of the Romanesque abbey, based on the 2001 survey. (Inset) detail of the plan of the north triforium showing (in black) the 12th-century openings and surviving fabric, later features in fine line, and (in grey) the areas cut out in the 13th century to accommodate the vaulting shafts. The depth of the removed fabric is unknown.

13th-century vault supports were made to match the string-course in the 13th century (**78**).

Above the triforium level there is a second string course, decorated with an alternating pattern of sunken and raised diamonds, which defined the base of the clerestory. The present clerestory passage is at 29.8m AOD and is presumably the Romanesque passage reused. The windows of the clerestory have been removed altogether by later fenestration, but to either side of the openings Romanesque fabric survives almost to the top of the wall at *c*.36.0 AOD. We have followed Wilson's suggested scheme for the windows, setting them high in the outer face of the wall to clear the roofs of the aisles. The inner face of the wall is cut away to form tall, stilted and round-headed openings each outlined with a continuous roll moulding. Sections of such a moulding have been reset to either side of several of the present (14th century) windows. *In situ* in the Romanesque fabric that flanks the windows there are the remains of tall, blind, lateral arches decorated with face-out chevron. Some of the voussoirs of the lateral arches survive to give an indication of the original height and width of these features. Springers of lower arches (forming arch-in-arch motifs within the lateral arches) have been observed in the passage on the south side.[1] The springers of these lower arches are *c*.1.70m above the level of the clerestory passage floor (*c*.1.60m in the two eastern bays of the nave) (**76, 80**).

The north aisle
The north aisle was originally intended to be quadrant-vaulted

80 North face of south clerestory passage showing a springer and voussoir for the lower arch in a lateral blind arch. *OC*

81 North aisle from the west. *AH*

1 Information M Thurlby, confirmed and recorded by Oliver Chamberlain, trainee mason, in February 2019; Hoey 1989, 85; Engel 2007, 97.

82A Nave, north aisle window, interior. *WD*

82B Nave north aisle windows, exterior. The shafts have been adapted and may originally have had capitals or been continuous rolls.

and remnants of this intention survive in the east bay of the north nave aisle (**51**); this plan was modified and the aisles built with rib vaulting (Wilson 1985, 73) (**75, 81**)[2]. Both the ribs and the transverse arches rise from the capitals of the nave piers on the inner side of the aisle, and stepped responds on the outer face of the aisle. The transverse arches are square in section with plain soffit faces, but all the vault ribs carry double roll mouldings. The respond capitals in the north nave are unusually complex and varied and are described more fully below (p89ff).

As noted above (p31) the inner elevations of the nave north aisle windows are assumed to

have retained their original form. On the inside they have chevron-decorated voussoirs and nook shafts with scalloped capitals (**82A**). However, on the outside the heads of these windows have been adapted in the 14th century. The voussoirs of the inner orders have been cut back to form single-splayed window-heads (**82B**). The flanking shafts have been heightened and now disappear into the window-heads. This could be an adaptation either of nook-shafts (the capitals having been removed) or of continuous rolls (**74**); in other words the windows could have had continuous rolls on the outside, nook shafts on the inside.

2 At Tewkesbury there are similar quadrant arches in the west walls of the transepts opening into the aisles, but there they are entirely separate from the aisle vaulting and seem to be intended to buttress the tower.

The south aisle

The south aisle was rebuilt in 1318 with large windows ornamented with ballflower and arched buttresses (**83, 84**) (Heighway 2012). The internal Romanesque responds were however retained, though they can be seen to be leaning outward.

Outside, the lowest 2m appears to be original Romanesque walling, with small blockwork and numerous Romanesque masons marks. If this walling is early 12th century, then it did not have strip buttresses. The nave clerestory *does* have strip buttresses, 85cm wide, decorated with vertical corner rolls and shapes that, in outline, look like a simple form of beakhead (**85, 86**). The eastern arm of the church can be seen to be inconsistent in the same way, with the upper part of the building above the lower of the two string courses having engaged half-round shafts as bay dividers while the walling below the lower string course has none (**1, 35**).

The west end

The Romanesque west end does not survive: the two western bays of the nave were entirely rebuilt in the 15th century. The eastern of these

83 South aisle from the west.

84 South aisle external view from the south-west after the completion of the restoration in 2013.

85 South aisle strip buttresses at clerestory level.

86 South aisle strip buttresses at clerestory level (detail looking east). The outward lean of the wall has been corrected above the 12th-century work.

87 The Romanesque western wall exposed in 2017.

two bays is the same width east-west as the other, Romanesque, bays and the western one is longer (about 6 metres).

St John Hope (Hope 1897, 121) explained this asymmetry by suggesting that the church had originally had an extra bay on the west and that the Romanesque church had been shortened in the 15th century by half a bay. He pointed out that the 12th-century outer parlour (west slype) had also been shortened, and he supposed that the Romanesque west front had originally aligned with a longer slype and had consisted of equal west bays.[3] F S Waller followed by Sir Alfred Clapham, suggested that the Romanesque west front was on the present line, as did McAleer (Welander 1991, 69-74; McAleer 1984, 192-202; 545-50).

Waller was proved correct in 2017 when the works associated with 'Project Pilgrim' uncovered a section of the western wall of the nave, slightly west of the present west front. The wall had two mortar types: the outside of small but even blockwork was bonded with orange mortar; the core of the wall was bonded with a very hard yellow mortar (**87,**

88). The section in front of the west door was not exposed so it was not possible to tell if the western door was recessed as at Tewkesbury. The remains of the orange-mortar wall were also seen next to the west slype (**92**).[4]

Nature of western wall

The western wall was of small blockwork. This is a wall-face, not a foundation (*pace* Morris 2017, 33), with medieval layers accumulated against it. The blockwork is similar to that of the lower part of the south aisle wall, which is also thought to be Romanesque (Heighway 2012, 22, fig3; above p64). Yet the stonework of the eastern arm is of ashlars. So the structure of the nave and west front was different from the eastern arm, though of course this difference would not have been evident to the observer at the time, as the smaller

3 The west slype/parlour has indeed been shortened, but the western bay was never more than half a bay long; see **2**, **3**, **92**, **104**.
4 Our observations were brief: we await a fuller publication from Borders Archaeology.

88 The Romanesque western wall exposed in 2017.

blockwork and perhaps the ashlars as well would have been rendered, plastered, and painted to resemble ashlar (cf Worcester: Guy 1994, 10-11).

A great Romanesque church begun in 1089 would have had a western façade of some splendour (McAleer 1984, 19). In England in the late 11th century some of the most important churches, Westminster, Canterbury, Durham, had façades with towers, one at the west end of each aisle. At Gloucester, it was in all probability a western tower that fell in 1164, and the *Historia* records the rebuilding of 'the west tower on the south side' in 1242.[5] There is even a 13th century drawing that might represent such towers.[6]

A two-tower façade at Gloucester is all the more likely because Tewkesbury abbey church (**89**), begun after 1087 and completed in the 1120s, with many elements modelled on Gloucester, was originally designed to have towers at the

west end of each aisle (Thurlby 1985a, 36). These were never completed, but the evidence of the intended design is still there, with the unfinished towers visible in the roof spaces (**90**; Thurlby 2003, 103). Tewkesbury also had a deeply recessed ordered entrance (**91**) and it is possible that Gloucester had the same style of western entrance, although in all likelihood more highly decorated (see below under Romanesque carving and decoration, p92, p95). Such an arrangement at the west end would provide an explanation of the bay asymmetry (**92**) (McAleer 1984, 199).

Physical evidence for at least a north-west tower at Gloucester can be seen in the north wall of the north aisle at the west end; it is 2.3m thick (this excludes the thickness of the parlour/slype wall). The thick wall is clearly visible at roof level, it returns to normal width 10m or more from the western parapet[7] (**93**), and probably represents the north wall of the tower.

5 Hare 1993b, 43; Barber 1998.
6 British Library Royal 13A III f.41v; Thomson *et al* 2011, 25, fig19. The drawing may depict the turrets of the transepts.

7 The thicker wall continues to the east for another two metres, although it has been reduced to form a buttress.

89 Tewkesbury abbey from the south-east.

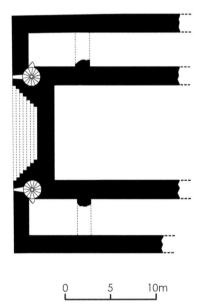

0   5   10m

90 Tewkesbury abbey: plan of western towers as visible in roof spaces above the aisles.

91 Tewkesbury abbey: west front.

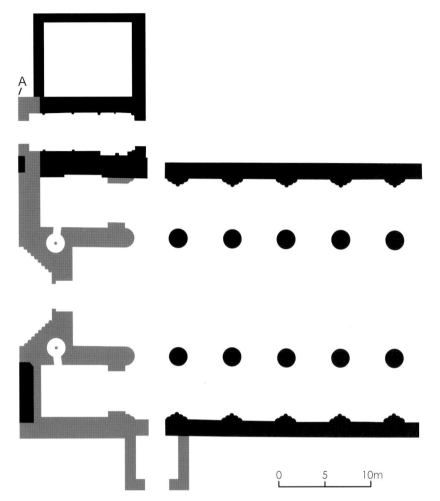

92 Gloucester abbey: plan of the west end showing surviving fabric (in black) including the foundations excavated in 2017 and reconstructed details (in grey). The western entrance follows the design of Tewkesbury though this is by no means certain. In the middle floor of the Church House 'loggia' (below p82) is a straight joint at the point marked 'A' on the plan.

The only other feature of the western towers is in the roof of the abbot's chapel in Church House. A doorway in the south wall (the north wall of the presumed tower) is used as the seating for one end of a 14th-century beam (**94**) (below p79 n4). The doorway was about 1.5m tall and 30cm wide and must once have opened onto the roof-leads of the chapel (**93**). In the interior, if this doorway passed right through the tower wall, it would have been below the first floor of the tower (below the level of the north aisle vault); we therefore suggest that it gave onto a wall passage and was accessed from a stair (similar to the arrangement for access to the room above the porch at Tewkesbury).

An additional piece of evidence for western towers remains just west of the south porch, where there is a redundant buttress, with a corresponding vault-shaft on the interior (**95**). The vault-shaft is bayed with the westernmost of the south aisle windows, and with the blind window above the porch, both late medieval. This must represent a 'first-phase' vaulting and fenestration arrangement[8] (later superseded by the present one) of two approximately equal bays at the west end of the south aisle. The position of the corresponding vault shaft on the north side of the south aisle is now within the span of the arcade arch, so it is clear that when this first-phase vaulting scheme was designed, there was a solid wall at this point on the north side of

8 Noted by McAleer 1984, 548, n136.

93 View north of Church House from the west end of the nave roof. The extra width of the parapet, representing the north wall of the north-west Romanesque tower, reduces to normal width towards the east on the right. *AFT*

94 Blocked doorway in the external north wall of the north-west tower now in the roof space above the abbot's chapel. *RKM*

the aisle, in other words a tower spur-wall (or an elongated pier) was still there at least on the south-west. The existence of this late survival of spur-wall (or elongated pier) implies that the 15th-century work was in two phases and that the first phase was an adaptation, not a rebuild, of the Romanesque west end.

The foundations of the spur-walls and therefore of the western towers was substantial. When excavations took place in the interior of the west end in 1939, the foundations of the aisle walls went down more than 10 feet.[9]

9 Cathedral library, *Clerk of Works Day Books*.

70

95 Two views of the west end of the south aisle showing the remaining portion and scar of the vaulting shaft (arrowed), and plan/diagram to show the position of the south aisle now-redundant buttress and interior shaft (in dark grey tone), indicating a first-phase 15th-century vault in the south aisle springing from a spur wall or elongated pier surviving from the proposed Romanesque arrangement (**92**).

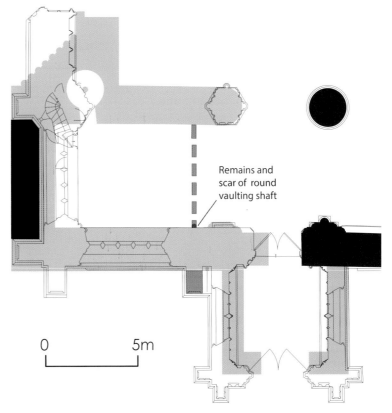

Remains and scar of round vaulting shaft

0   5m

71

96 Blocked arch at west end of north aisle, view north.

The internal wall face at the western end of the north aisle, and that in the nave and south aisle, are not in alignment. This could imply that the south-west tower was replaced at a different time from the north-west one. The whole process of rebuilding the west end may thus have been a piecemeal one: the present unified appearance being the last and most thorough alteration, presumably to be attributed to Abbot Morwent.

There is some enigmatic apparently Romanesque walling on the internal face of the north wall of the supposed north-west tower. Here there is the outline of a round arch (**96**). The centre of the arch shape is filled with small blockwork of Romanesque type: the wall to the west of the arch is in much larger blocks usually identified as late medieval. The arch does not accord with the present vaulting — it has its centre slightly west of that vaulting. The arch is unlikely to have been a window, because it is mostly obstructed externally by the building to the north, the 12th-century 'abbot's chapel'. We interpret this as a blind Romanesque arch, in the north wall of the north-west tower base, which was filled at an unknown date with re-used Romanesque masonry; the masonry into which the arch

was set being refaced during one of the late medieval alterations.[10] There is no certainty that the arch represents a Romanesque feature; it has nevertheless been included in the Romanesque plan (**3, 97**).

The ground plans of Gloucester and Tewkesbury (**97**) are very similar, though Gloucester has wider nave aisles in proportion to the nave span. Tewkesbury had near-square western tower bays at ground floor level but the bays were rectangular in the roof space (**79**) because there the western wall is much narrower. Now that we know the Gloucester western wall was on the present-day line, it is clear that the western aisle bays at Gloucester were also rectangular (cf McAleer 1984, 548): the similarity with Tewkesbury is therefore even more marked.

South porch

The south aisle was rebuilt starting in 1318; the Romanesque elevation being replaced with windows with two-centred arches, 'butterfly'

10 Welander (1991, 73) suggested that the west side of the arch represented the line of the last Norman respond. McAleer (1984, 550) suggested that the 12th-century infill masonry was re-used.

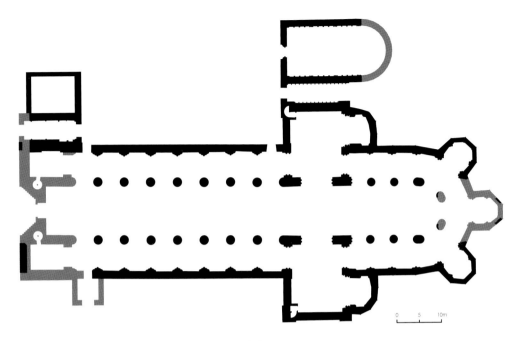

Gloucester St Peter's Abbey: the Romanesque ground plan

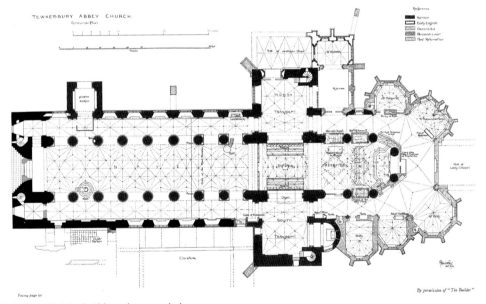

Tewkesbury St Mary's Abbey: the ground plan

97 Gloucester and Tewkesbury abbeys: comparative plans. Tewkesbury plan from *The Builder*, 1894: at the same scale.

tracery, and much use of ballflower decoration. This work can be seen to terminate at a near-vertical straight-joint east of the 15th-century south porch. The fact that it was not possible to complete the first window next to the porch suggests that in 1318 an earlier porch stood on this line (**3, 95**): there may thus have been a Romanesque porch in roughly the position of the present one (and therefore of course a south door).

ROMANESQUE CLAUSTRAL BUILDINGS

The cloister has Romanesque buildings on all four sides, establishing the original cloister outline (**3, 98**).

The inner parlour

The monk's inner parlour, where necessary conversation was allowed, is usually termed the east slype (**99**). In 1976 it was converted into the Treasury, and is now entered from the north transept through a modern opening in the north wall. It was a barrel-vaulted passageway without transverse arches with blind arcades on both sides. Neither side appears to have had a bench. The arcades to the south have free-standing shafts

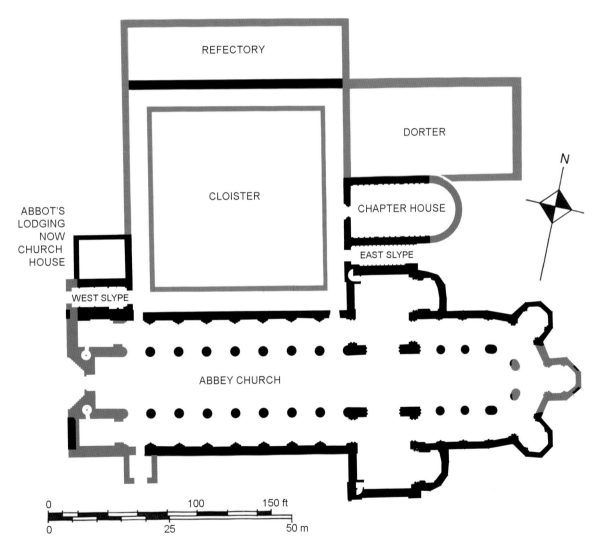

98 Gloucester abbey: plan of the Romanesque church and outline of claustral buildings.

topped with scallop capitals built over the plinth of the north transept; they are set on stepped plinths which have apparently been repaired in brick. The arcade on the north side today has a wooden bench which hides any evidence of benches, but old photographs show it has deep plinths with no sign of a bench (Welander 1991, 320). There is a good deal of paint still visible especially on the north arcades (below, p87). When initially built the passage was only the length of the north side of the transept, but it was extended in the 14th century. Before then it opened into the cloister: it was closed off at the rebuilding of the cloister in the late 14th century, then reopened via a door in 1874 (Welander 1991, 321, 455, 480).

The chapter house
The chapter house was originally built in the late 11th century: signs of fire-reddening on its western wall suggest that it had to be rebuilt and its present form is perhaps early 12th century (**100, 101, 102**). The original chapter house had three equal-sized arches at the west end:

101 The chapter house interior, looking west. Inset (A) shows the surviving cushion capital from the earlier west façade. *Main photograph: AH. Inset detail: WD*

A

one cushion capital survives (**101**A). The rebuilt western façade had a four-order central arch with chevron, flanked by windows with nook shafts but no chevron. The roof is barrel-vaulted with slightly pointed transverse arches on recessed semicircular wall-shafts with scalloped capitals, and double shafts on the chord of the apse (**100**). Between the shafts is blind arcading in groups of four with paired responds, also with scalloped capitals. The first two arcades from the east on each side employed chevron on the arch.

The east end was converted in the 14th century to a rectangular form but originally it was apsidal (Welander 1991, 325).[1]

1 We are told by Nick Hilyer that masonry perhaps of the original apsidal end is preserved under the stage: we have not surveyed this.

The dorter

Nothing is known of the 12th-century dorter. It may have occupied the usual position aligned north-south on the east side of the cloister (Welander 1991, 324), but when it was rebuilt in the 14th century it was aligned east-west — its south wall still carries the jamb of a window with ball-flower ornament. In either case there was no space for a night stair, the way being blocked by the lofty chapter house.

102 The chapter house, external façade.

The refectory

Although the refectory was rebuilt in the 13th century, excavations by St John Hope established that the undercroft was Norman and that it extended under the passage which now leads to the infirmary; that is, it occupied the whole of the north side of the cloister (Hope 1897, 110).

The outer parlour or locutorium

The outer parlour of the abbey is today usually termed the west slype (**103**). It is a 12th-century barrel-vaulted passage with flattened transverse ribs (similar in profile to those in the chapter house) on wall shafts with scallop capitals. In the east bay there has clearly been some disruption perhaps resulting from a vault failure — some of the capitals are re-used from other positions

and extra ribs have been inserted.[2] The slype sloped up from west to east: the capitals also rise in height.[3] The moulded round-arched west entrance is of early 13th-century form. The inner Perpendicular doorway is deeply recessed with several orders and partly covers the shafts and rib of the westernmost transverse arch; this rib is complete and not a termination; a similar situation is evident in the chapel above. The passage has clearly been shortened. In 2017 what could have been the original termination of the slype was observed (**104**). The wall (A on the plan) was built with a yellow mortar similar

2 GCAR 91/C.
3 The slype floor at the west end is at 12.6m AOD, at the east end 13m AOD, and the cloister still higher, at 14.7m AOD.

103 The west slype (*locutorium*). View to east. *AH*

to that in the core of the church's western wall foundations. It was also in line with the west face of the abbey church. If the identification is correct, then the westernmost bay of the slype was about half the length of the other bays.

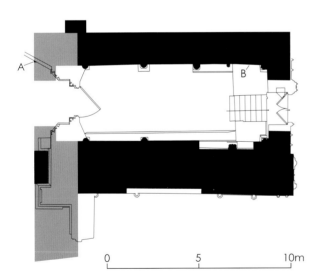

104 The west slype showing the surviving Romanesque structure (in black), the original west wall (in light grey) and the current doorways (in fine line). A fragment of what may be the original west wall of the west slype was revealed at 'A' under the wall of Church House during excavations in 2017.

At the east end of the slype on the north side is a blocked doorway or blind arch (B on the plan). The north wall here is 1.7m thick. The sill of the 'doorway' is at 14.3m AOD, about 0.5m below the level of the cloister. This is 1.5m above the basement of the adjacent 'abbot's tower' and more than 2m below the middle floor which might be supposed to be the abbot's quarters. If this was access for the abbot, the stairs would have been extremely steep.

The abbot's chapel

The room above the slype was probably the abbot's chapel, of *c*.1120-35 (**105, 106**). The interior has a barrel vault with three equal bays and one shorter west bay; the vault is supported by transverse arches on wall-shafts with scalloped capitals. The easternmost, terminal, shafts are square with angle-rolls, above which are square abaci with concave mouldings.[4] These support a

4 The roof aligns east-west on the west, and north to south at the east end (**93**). The east-west alignment must once have extended over the whole building. Subsequently there must have been a collapse, perhaps that which caused the alterations in the slype below. The eastern end of the roof was then rebuilt to align north-south: dendrochronology suggests this happened in the 14th century (Moir 2018).

105 Church House, abbot's chapel; looking west.

106 Church House, abbot's chapel, looking east.

vertical vault shaft, also with an angle-roll, which rises up into the barrel vault. The next pair of capitals have scallops ornamented with a five-lobed leaf at the corners; the other two pairs further west have plain scallop capitals. In the early 19th century the walls were observed to be lime-washed and painted to imitate masonry (Haines 1867, 53).

The chapel is just over a metre wider than the slype below: this means the chapel extends over the north wall of the slype which must be, on the ground floor, more than 1.5m thick.

West of the western pair of columns is a short bay of the barrel vault — about 0.7m — which terminates at the western wall with its late medieval window. There are no terminal shafts,

and evidently the room, like the slype below, has been shortened. The northern column of the last western pair of shafts stands in the stair-well at the entrance, and so its base is visible. This column is not an engaged half-shaft like the others - its lower part is three quarters round and its plinth is oddly angled, suggesting that there has always been an entrance at this point. Excessive wear near the column base also suggests this, as well as a slight curvature in the side profile of the same column which might indicate a doorway.[5]

5 When the room was refurbished in 1863, signs of the 'original Saxon entrance' (implying a round headed arch), were found: *The Builder*, April 25 1863. There is no indication of the position of this door.

80

107 Church House, western external elevation. *MT*

The 12th-century abbot's tower

The 'abbot's tower' is part of a larger complex called Church House (**98, 107**). It is a rectangular three-storey tower *c.*1130-50 judging by the decoration. From the 14th century it was part of the prior's lodging and in post-medieval times the deanery. The entire building was remodelled, probably in the 16th century, in part reusing Romanesque and later architectural material; it was heavily restored in 1863 (Morriss 2002, 77-78). It is now used as diocesan offices. The tower has plentiful chevron and billet decoration arranged in vertical strips on either side of each window opening; the decoration is in vertical alignment on all three floors (**108**). Also on each floor is a small doorway at the east end which might have been the access to a garderobe (in which case a date is indicated at which gardrobes would have been acceptable: no later than the early 17th century (Morriss 2002, 77-78).[6]

6 Carter and Basire (1807) show a rectangular structure on the outside which might have been the remnant of this garderobe.

81

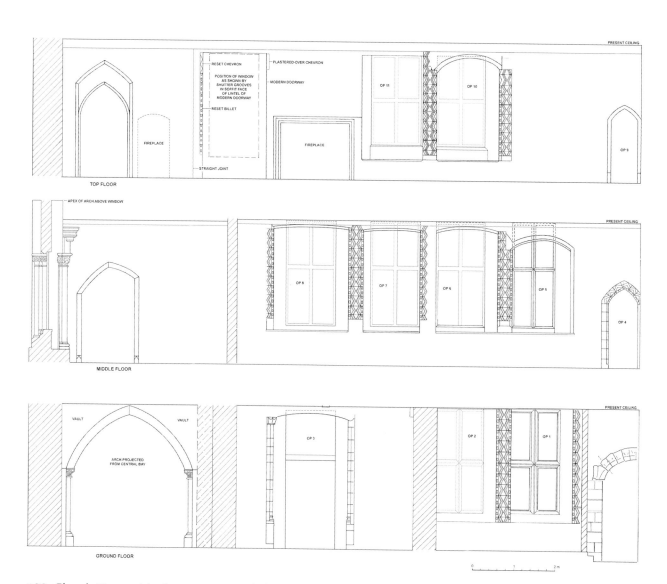

108 Church House: abbot's tower: measured sketch of interior elevation of the north wall.
Original drawing C Heighway, emended by R Bryant.

The 'loggia'

West of the tower was added a late 12th-century[7] three-storey building which originally had two open arches on the ground floor (**107**). Its gable has five tall shallow round-headed panels with chevron ornament. This gable is likely to have been reused and reset from the original west gable of the tower.

7 judging by the stiff-leaf capitals inside and the simple groin vault: pers. comm. Malcolm Thurlby.

The abbot's tower: Romanesque detail

The core structure is the abbot's tower itself. Some of the 12th-century decoration may survive *in situ* (**108, 109, 110**A, B, C). Two of the carved window jambs on the top floor are disturbed 1.9m above the sill; above this the decoration changes in each case. The splays are odd, alternating straight-sided and angled, but done in the same way on each floor. We think (*pace* Morriss 2002, 77-8) that the alterations of the 16th century adapted the 12th-century window openings; and that the

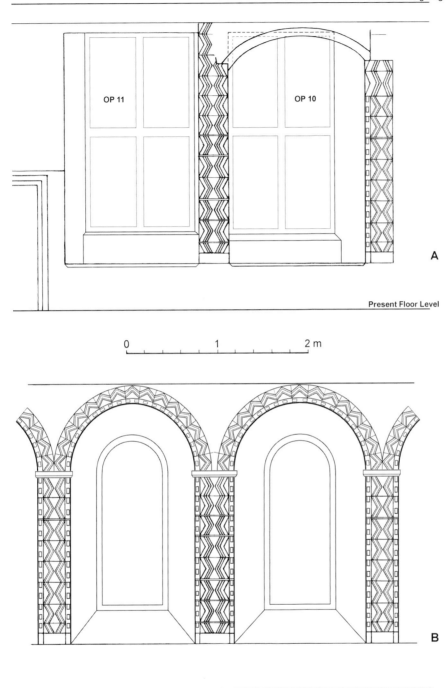

Present Ceiling Height

OP 11

OP 10

A

Present Floor Level

0   1   2 m

B

109 Church House: abbot's tower: (A) present elevation of two top-floor windows
(B) reconstruction of the two windows incorporating *in situ* decorated jambs, as well as
chevron-with-billet voussoirs re-used above the north-east doorways on the middle (interior)
(**110**E) and upper (exterior) floors.

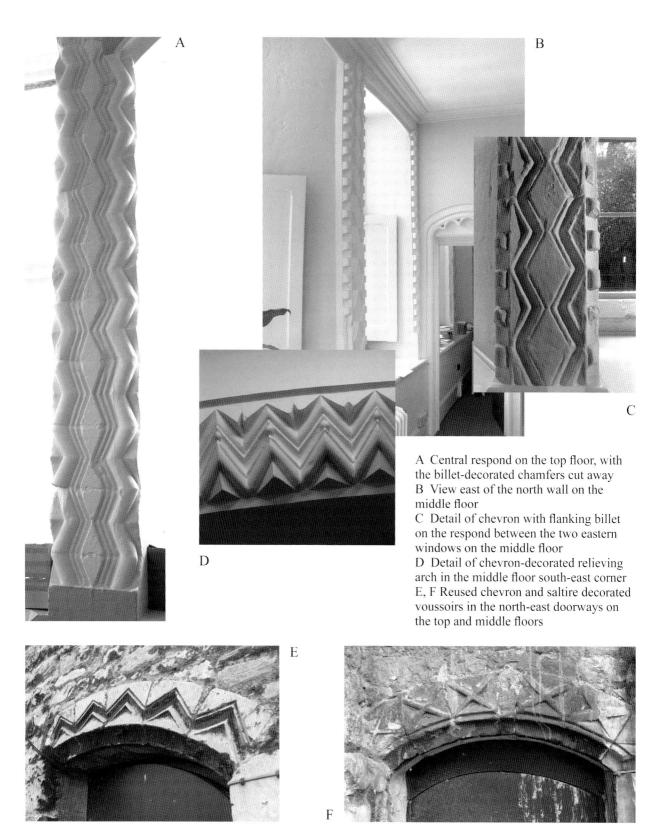

A Central respond on the top floor, with the billet-decorated chamfers cut away
B View east of the north wall on the middle floor
C Detail of chevron with flanking billet on the respond between the two eastern windows on the middle floor
D Detail of chevron-decorated relieving arch in the middle floor south-east corner
E, F Reused chevron and saltire decorated voussoirs in the north-east doorways on the top and middle floors

110 12th-century *in situ* and re-used carved decoration in the abbot's tower, Church House.

windows were originally round-headed (**109**); voussoirs with chevron-and-billet decoration were later re-set on the doorways to the garderobe (**110**E). From the outside the northern elevation is unexceptional (**111**): it has been completely refaced (perhaps twice, once in the 16th century and again in 1863).

The abbot's tower may therefore represent one of the earliest high-status dwellings in the country, and deserves to be better known. There are many questions still to be answered about this Romanesque building: why, for instance, is there decoration on the ground floor (the basement, in relation to ground surfaces to the east); how was it accessed (presumably by an external stair); why is one opening on the two lower floors wider than the others; and why are there bracing or relieving arches on the south-west and south-east corners on the ground floor, and on the south-east corner of the middle floor?

St Mary's Gate

Although not one of the claustral buildings, it seems important to include here St Mary's Gate (**112**), the principal access to the abbey on the west side of the precinct. The gate takes its name from the nearby Anglo-Saxon foundation of St

111 Church House, northern external elevation.

112 St Mary's Gate (looking west) showing freestanding chevron on the transverse rib.
MT

Mary de Lode. (Until the widening of College Street in the late 19th century, the only other access to the abbey was via the two narrow lanes leading to small gates in the south wall of the precinct.) In origin St Mary's gate must have been a Romanesque structure, but the only remnant of this period is the vault of the inner bays of the gate which has a central transverse arch decorated with freestanding chevron work (Welander 1991, 101; Morriss 2002 59-62). The chevron is of a later type not found elsewhere in the precinct.

ROMANESQUE POLYCHROMY

There is enough surviving internal poly-chromy to indicate that the original building was brightly decorated. Obviously the traces have been overlaid many times and there is always the possibility of confusion with later schemes. However Tristam recorded various instances of Romanesque painted decoration. 'A pier on the south side of the choir displays a treatment of a massive type, characteristic of early 12th-century work. The ground, ochre-coloured, is divided into very large [fictive] blocks of masonry, with joints, about an inch wide, painted and outlined in red. The round moulding of the necking is covered with diagonal bands of yellow ochre and white, separated by black lines. The bell of the capital, which is [painted] black, is divided into large square blocks of masonry by joints similar to those on the shafts, but here painted vermilion. The abacus is ochre-coloured and in the cavetto moulding are painted roundels.' (Tristam 1944, 125) (**113**A, **114, 115**). He mentions that the abaci of the capitals of the nave piers are decorated with a red chevron pattern (not now discernible): also that the 'abbot's cloister' (the east slype) wall-arcade arches have their voussoirs indicated by a double line and the white blocks 'marbled' with semi-circular brush strokes (**113**B).

In 1992 several voussoirs from a Romanesque opening were extracted from the fill of the 14th-century altar in the south-east ambulatory chapel (Heighway 1993, 25; **41**). When originally ex-

A   B

113 A: Pier on the south side of the choir. B: Voussoirs in the north arcade of the east slype: illustrations in Tristram 1944.

114 Romanesque polychromy on one of the piers of the choir with inset detail. *RA*

cavated these carried fictive ashlars done in whitewash and red paint.

The abbot's chapel also once carried fictive ashlars in red paint (above p80).

There are traces of red paint depicting ashlars on the piers of the crypt; again, it is not clear whether this represents later work.

It is worth mentioning that at Gloucester the internal paint schemes have been applied directly onto the stone, without an underlying plaster layer.

There would once have been external rendering which would have carried a layer of plaster, also painted with red lines to represent ashlars. Excavations on the exterior of the west front are rumoured to have noted traces of white plaster – similar external decoration has been recorded at Worcester (Barker and Romain 2001, 9; Guy 1994, 10-11) and York (Philips 1985, 100 and plate 73).

115 Romanesque polychromy (fictive ashlars) on one of the choir piers. *MT*

ROMANESQUE CARVING AND DECORATION

At St Peter's Abbey, Gloucester the decoration of the earliest Romanesque phases is generally restrained. There is, however, a small group of carvings that deserve to be noted, together with architectural decoration (capitals, springers and voussoirs). Some of this material is still *in situ* in the 12th-century fabric, while other items now form part of the catalogued collection of carved stones and fragments in the cathedral stone store. Richard Morris (2004, 9-12) has identified 41 of these as Romanesque; one more has been included since his inventory was completed.

Sculptural carving

There are nine carvings that are sculptural in quality (**116**). Three take the form of grotesque animal heads and can be seen *in situ* near the western end of the nave arcade. Two of these are wide-mouthed, bulbous-eyed creatures that act as corbels which support later vaulting shafts (**116** A, B). The third is a smaller, large-eyed animal mask at the centre of the hood moulding on the westernmost 12th-century arch in the northern nave arcade. The creature holds the stems of two grape clusters in its mouth (**116** C). A crouching, wide-mouthed, heavily-maned lion still survives as the gable finial on the north transept (**116** D, E). On a corbel in the north-west corner of the chapter house there is a pair of strange, upside-down creatures with pointed ears, elliptical eyes, wide curving mouths and folded wings that might perhaps be bats (**116** F) (this carving was published upside down in Welander 1991, 83). A rather weathered animal-head label stop has been reset on the hood moulding of the 14th-century east window of the south transept (**116** G), and the muzzle of a second animal-head label stop (with a human head gripped in its sharp teeth) survives

as a loose fragment (**116** H, I). There are also two large, rounded, wide-mouthed grotesque animal-heads, one a label stop from a double-springer (**116** J, K), and the other a corbel or label stop (**116** L) (now in St John's cathedral, Newfoundland)[1] that has been compared to the group of grotesque heads on the apse boss at Kilpeck in Herefordshire (Chwojko and Thurlby 1997, 18, pls. IVc and IVd). All of these carvings would fit happily into the repertoire of carving from the late 11th or first quarter of the 12th century.

Decorated capitals

The free-standing columns in the central vessel of the 11th-century crypt have volute capitals, in a style which is not carried up into the super-structure of the church. Two of these capitals are carved, one with a moustached face (**8, 117** A) and the other with small, vertical, foliated panels (**7, 117** B, C). A simple volute capital in the stone store is probably, by association, also late 11th century (**117** D).

Almost all the other capitals in the church are cushion or scallop capitals. However, the respond capitals in the north aisle of the nave are more decorated and more varied. Most of these are versions of the scallop capitals found elsewhere, but with a wide range of different details — plain and sheathed cones, flat and hollowed shields, upward-pointed 'blades' on the corners and in one case a vertical leaf in the centre of the front face. There are also capitals with interlace, a foliated volute capital, and a capital with 'sunken' volutes that are hollowed-out of the face. The two capitals nearest to the door into the cloister are the most highly decorated.

---

1 Photograph and information provided by Malcolm Thurlby.

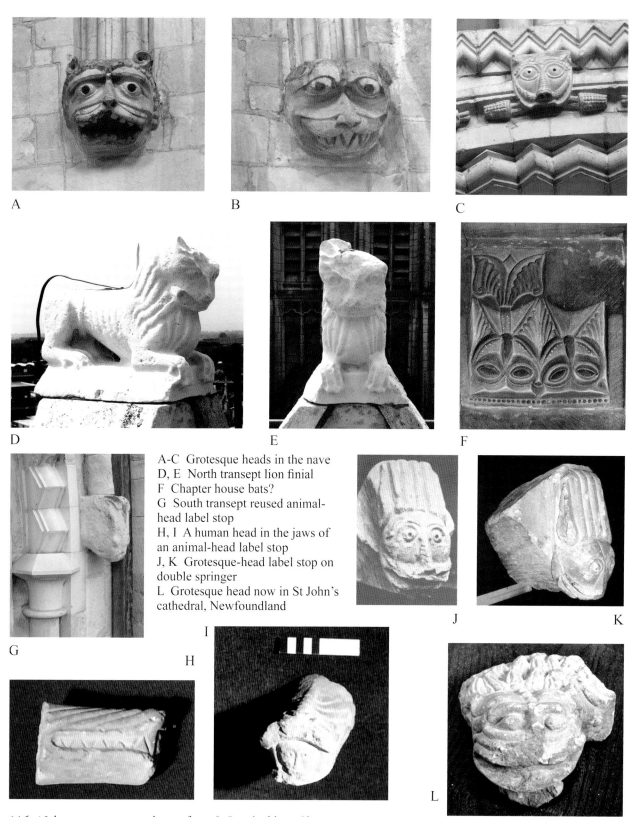

A-C Grotesque heads in the nave
D, E North transept lion finial
F Chapter house bats?
G South transept reused animal-
head label stop
H, I A human head in the jaws of
an animal-head label stop
J, K Grotesque-head label stop on
double springer
L Grotesque head now in St John's
cathedral, Newfoundland

116 12th-century stone sculpture from St Peter's abbey, Gloucester.

A-C Volute capitals from the crypt
D Engaged volute capital
E Bay 6 north aisle respond capital
F Bay 6 north aisle respond capital west face
G Bay 7 north aisle respond capital
H Engaged decorated capital, possibly from
the west end of church

117 Late 11th-century and early 12th-century carved capitals from St Peters abbey Gloucester.

One is covered by a riot of interlacing plant stems, with clusters of rounded leaves and spiral-tipped tendrils (**117** G). The other capital carries foliate decoration in low relief outlined with fine incised lines (**117** E). The corners of this capital are defined by stemmed volutes, while each side face carries round-leafed palmettes rising from a collar between two volutes (**117** F). The north aisle capitals belongs to the final phase of the construction of the nave probably *c.* 1120, and aspects of their carving may offer a tantalising glimpse into the decoration of the now lost west end.

A highly decorated, engaged capital in the stone store may also have come from the west end (Morris 2004, 10, 17/023). Two faces of the capital are carved with multi-scallops, with the shields consisting of interlocking pelleted inverted arches, and with vertical serrated leaves in between the cones of each scallop (**117** H). The upper part of the abacus for this capital carries a single row of tiny chevron or saw-tooth in shallow relief.

Carved decoration reused architecturally in the standing structure

Gloucester abbey is renowned for its 14th-century re-use in *architectural* ways of earlier, usually 12th-century, decoration. Examples of this include shafts, capitals, and bases, as well as mouldings used to decorate reinforcing 'bracers', all in the choir tribune (**28, 29, 30**). On the outside of the 14th-century choir there are considerable quantities of Romanesque shafts and capitals (**44-5**). The south transept has re-used columns and bases on the east and west elevations (**61**), as well as the 14th-century south façade (**58**), which we consider to incorporate much of the decoration of the Romanesque version.

The 14th-century masons were not averse to carving stone in an antique style on the occasions where their supply of re-usable decoration gave out. Ashwell cited examples of chevron being carved for the south transept elevation, where the masons created multiple chevron on a single stone (Ashwell 1985, 115). On the north transept gable one of the T-mouldings was created from an old Romanesque roll-moulding (Heighway 2007b, 2), and on the choir roof-space windows the masons went to the trouble of manufacturing window-heads which matched in dimension (but not this time in style) the re-used Romanesque window-jambs (GCAR 93/H).

Re-used chevron appears on the 'bridge', known as the 'whispering gallery' at the east end, which gave access from one gallery ambulatory to the other after the building of the great east window in the 14th century. When the Lady Chapel was built in the late 15th century the 'bridge' also provided access to the upper story chapel. The reused chevron comes from a range of blind arcade arches; as reset, they are 30 cm wide, 120 cm tall and with 30cm wide jambs (**118** A, B). There are five arches on each 'bridge'; those on the north are all lateral-to-face chevron. Half those on the south are also lateral chevron, with the remaining two and a half face-frontal chevron. Apparently there was insufficient chevron to complete the south side, which implies there was not much lateral chevron available. The origin of this chevron is unknown.[2] Perhaps it came from the crossing tower, which was completely demolished in the 14th century (see p51) and could have been decorated, as was Tewkesbury (**89**).

Re-used Romanesque material in Church House (**110**) is inserted at a much later date, perhaps 16th century, but it includes some items unknown elsewhere in the abbey. A doorhead is made from voussoirs carrying saltires and a hollow chamfer (**110** F). Also in Church House,

2 Wilson thought that the 'bridge' decoration derived from a rebuilding of the choir in the early 12th century. He claimed it was the same size as the plain arcading which survives on the choir. However, the choir arcading is wider and lower (44cm wide and 95cm high) and each bay is divided from the next by a shaft *c.* 12cm wide).

A South

B North

C

D

G

J

E

H I

K

F

A, B Reused chevron on the Lady Chapel bridge
C-E Carved stones probably from a decorative frieze
F Stone from a vault rib with decoration similar to C-E
G-I Voussoirs decorated with chevron and pellet or ball ornament from an opening *c*.90cm wide.
J Engaged shaft with spiral decoration of strings of small pellets divided by rolls
K, L Chevron-outlined lozenges enclosing cruciform leaves with delicate spiral-tipped tendrils

L

118 Re-used chevron in the Lady Chapel 'bridge' and carved decoration in the cathedral stone store.

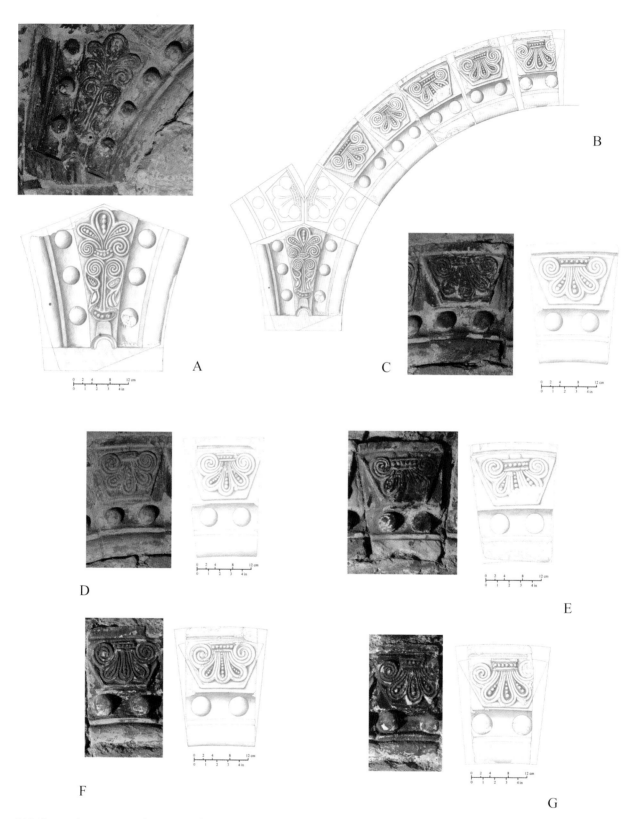

119 Re-used springer and voussoirs from the north-east doorway on the ground floor of the abbot's tower, Church House.

on the ground floor and middle floor there are internal relieving arches, two of which carry reused chevron; the one on the middle floor being of an unusual type which includes a pellet within each upward-pointing zig-zag (**110** D).

Another doorhead is constructed from a 12th-century double springer and five voussoirs (**119**); these are carved with foliate decoration, with a heavy inner edge moulding and a hollow chamfer in which there are large round pellets like the abacus of one of the north aisle capitals. The foliate decoration on the Church House pieces is also very closely paralleled on this north aisle capital, supporting a date of *c.*1120. The springer and voussoirs came from a double opening (**119** B), and the decoration is unlike any of the other carved stones *in situ* or re-used in Church House. It has been suggested (Bryant 2017) that these stones therefore came from somewhere else in the abbey and that they may have been part of a *pulpitum* screen or perhaps the arcade of the 12th-century cloister.

Other carved decoration

All still-usable stone was recycled wherever possible by the medieval masons, and almost every repair project produces examples of Romanesque stone re-used as rubble or ashlar, some of which carries decoration not found elsewhere in the building. For instance, built into the 14th-century upper walls of the nave clerestory are thirteen blocks of stone with recessed circles with radii of 70-75 mm (**120**). There are four types of design, which can be reassembled to form a steep gable (though other reconstructions are possible). The circles may have been located on the west front and/or the western towers, or, since they are quite un-weathered, may have decorated liturgical furniture. Recessed circles

seem to be rare in England though they are known occasionally in France, for instance at Lyon, Poitiers, and Auxerre (Bagshaw 2002a, 12-14).

Twenty of the 42 Romanesque stones in the stone store collection have geometric or foliate carving. Thirteen are carved with chevron. Four of the stones are voussoirs from an opening *c.* 90 cm wide and the inward-pointing chevron creates lozenges down the centre of the soffit faces (eg **118** G-I). These stones also have hollow chamfers with round pellet or ball ornament along each arris, and chevron on one outer face. The use of large round pellets in the hollow chamfer is first found in the standing fabric at Gloucester on the previously-mentioned respond capital towards the west end of the north aisle (**117** E, F). There are also two stones where chevron-edged lozenges enclose delicate cruciform leaves with a central boss and slender, spiral-tipped side shoots (**118** K, L). Three stones from an ornamental frieze (**118** C-E) and a stone from a vault rib (**118** F) are carved with curve-sided diamonds within a circle, a motif also found at Old Sarum and elsewhere (King 1986, 26-7, 37 n27).

Morris suggested that the chevron, together with the capital (**117** H) discussed above, the stones from the vault rib and the ornamental frieze, and an attached shaft decorated with continuous spirals of beading separated by rolls (**118** J) might belong to 'a lost major portal, such as the processional east door from the cloister or the west door of the nave'. He adds: 'The wide range of motifs displayed illustrates the importance of the abbey as a centre for the rich sculptural output of craftsmen in the Cotswolds (e.g. Elkstone) and the Herefordshire School in the half-century between *c.*1110-20 and *c.*1160-70' (Morris 2004, 10).

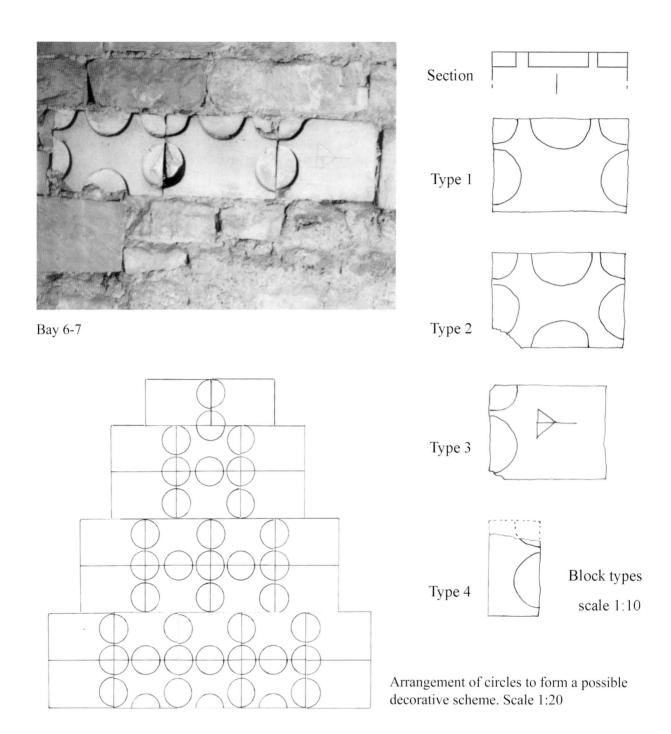

Bay 6-7

Section

Type 1

Type 2

Type 3

Type 4

Block types
scale 1:10

Arrangement of circles to form a possible
decorative scheme. Scale 1:20

120 Re-used circle decoration in the nave roof space in the upper part of the 14th-century north wall.

SOURCES AND ASSOCIATIONS OF THE ROMANESQUE ABBEY CHURCH OF ST PETER AT GLOUCESTER

Malcolm Thurlby

The immediate context for Serlo's abbey church of St Peter's Gloucester is the great rebuilding of cathedral and abbey churches that followed the Norman Conquest.[1] Even before 1066, Edward the Confessor's Westminster Abbey was built in a Norman style, a change from the Anglo-Saxon tradition which did not escape the attention of the keen architectural eye of the twelfth-century chronicler William of Malmesbury (d. 1143).[2] After the Conquest the Anglo-Saxon church of the cathedral-monastery of Christ Church, Canterbury, was rebuilt between 1070 and 1077 by the newly appointed Archbishop Lanfranc. Lanfranc's design was modelled on William the Conqueror's abbey church of Saint-Étienne at Caen where Lanfranc had been abbot before taking up the appointment at Canterbury. The new cathedral was no larger than its Anglo-Saxon predecessor but the Norman style was quite distinct from Anglo-Saxon churches and from those in Lotharingia and the Holy Roman Empire. In or before 1073 work also commenced on the Benedictine abbey church of St Augustine's, Canterbury, which features an apse-ambulatory plan with radiating chapels above a groin-vaulted crypt, a crossing tower, aisleless transepts with two-storey eastern chapels, a nave flanked by aisles, and twin western towers, all features in common with St Peter's Gloucester.[3] It may be significant that the

work at St Augustine's was undertaken for Abbot Scotland (1070-1087) who, like Abbot Serlo, was previously a monk at Le Mont Saint-Michel.[4] A large crypt under the eastern arm was designed at Winchester cathedral (1079), Bury St Edmunds abbey (1081), Evesham abbey (in or soon after 1078), Worcester cathedral (1084) and Old St Paul's cathedral, London.[5] Of these, Worcester is the most significant (**121**) in that it presages many of the elements at Gloucester including the three-bay presbytery* with an apse-ambulatory plan and three polygonal radiating chapels raised above the crypt, a complex groin vault in the apse of the crypt as in the transept chapels at Gloucester, a round-headed gallery arcade on columnar piers which were probably also used for the main arcades, groin-vaulted aisles, two-storey transept chapels, aisleless transepts with vices in the outer western corners, and lateral porches in the nave (north at Worcester and south at Gloucester).[6] The three-bay presbytery with columnar piers was probably used earlier at Evesham Abbey but without an apse-ambulatory plan. The list of common features suggests that the design of St Peter's Gloucester was inspired by Wulfstan's cathedral at Worcester — not surprising given that St Peter's abbey was within the see. Moreover, whilst Serlo probably introduced the customs of Le Mont Saint-Michel at Gloucester, liturgically

---

* The term 'choir' is preferred elsewhere in this book.
1 Fernie 2000, 19-33; Gem 1988.
2 Gem 1981; Fernie 2000, 96-8.
3 For the western towers at Gloucester see above p67.

4 Gem 1982, 1-2.
5 For Evesham see Cox 2010, 26; for Old St Paul's, see Gem 1990.
6 Gem 1978, 34; Guy 1994, 59-65. Large columnar piers for the main arcades also occur in the nave at Shrewsbury abbey (1083) and Malvern priory (1085), and in the nave gallery at Shrewsbury.

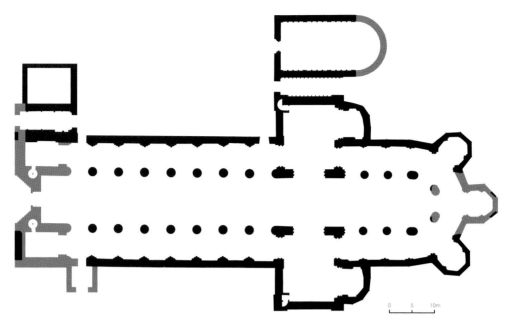

Gloucester St Peter's Abbey: the Romanesque ground plan

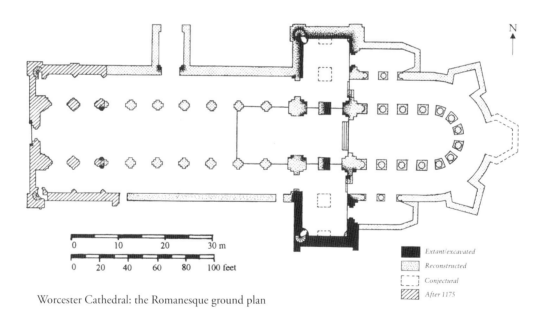

Extant/excavated
Reconstructed
Conjectural
After 1175

Worcester Cathedral: the Romanesque ground plan

121 The Romanesque ground plans of Gloucester abbey and Worcester cathedral priory compared. Worcester taken from Engel 2007, fig8, based on the archaeology archive at Worcester. The plan of the polygonal chapels at Worcester is assumed to be the same as the excavated crypt chapel.

Gloucester also shows native influences which could have originated at Worcester where the Anglo-Saxon tradition of the *Regularis Concordia* continued after the Conquest.[7]

Nevertheless it is far from being a model-copy relationship. The three-sided termination of the Gloucester presbytery arcade is different from Worcester, as is the geometry of the polygonal outer ambulatory wall and the radiating chapels. The segmental arches in the Gloucester crypt are quite different from the round-headed arches in the crypt at Worcester — the result of the three-aisle arrangement at Gloucester rather than the four aisles of the central space at Worcester. The three-aisle plan is presaged in the crypt of Evesham abbey.[8]

The bishop's chapel at Hereford, constructed for Robert the Lotharingian, 1079-95, may have inspired many features of Gloucester abbey.[9] These include the segmental arches of the Gloucester crypt, the quadrant vaults in the presbytery (tribune) gallery with their arches carried on single shaft responds with round bases and cushion capitals without abaci, the presbytery high vault, and the ashlar masonry and double-splay windows in the Gloucester crypt. It is doubtless significant that it was the bishop of Hereford, Robert the Lotharingian, who laid the first stone of Serlo's church.[10]

Another motif reminiscent of Worcester cathedral occurs in the south nave clerestory at Gloucester, namely a lower arch of the same width within the jambs of a higher arch (**76**, **80**), as reconstructed by Richard Gem in the Worcester transept.[11] Both Gloucester and Tewkesbury included a main arcade and gallery in the presbytery, albeit with different articulation, and something similar followed slightly later at Pershore abbey.[12] The crossing piers elongated on an east-west axis have the same plan at Gloucester and Tewkesbury with plain north and south responds, and paired half shafts on the east and west responds. Plain north and south responds are also found on the elongated crossing piers at Great Malvern priory, founded in 1085.[13] Thus the walls of the internal faces of the crossing piers facilitate the setting of choir stalls flat against the walls, an eminently practical solution to the continuation of the choir stalls through the crossing into the nave. This solution may have been invented at Great Malvern, Gloucester or Tewkesbury.

Gloucester and Tewkesbury had a high vault in the presbytery which possibly included ribs in the apse as in the ground floor of the south transept chapel at Tewkesbury. Pershore abbey had barrel-vaulted transepts and concomitantly a vaulted choir and probably a nave high vault. A high rib vault was used in the nave of Chepstow priory, founded 1067-71, so the presbytery there would have been vaulted, although the form of that vault is not known. The quadrant vaults in Tewkesbury nave aisles are similar to those over the presbytery (tribune) gallery at Gloucester and as originally intended in the nave aisles at Gloucester (**15**, **51**, above p62-3). The upper external blind arcades of the transepts and nave of Tewkesbury have been allied with examples in western France where, like Tewkesbury, they frequently accompany barrel-vaulted interiors.[14] A barrel vault is suggested for the presbytery and transepts of Gloucester (above p22-3, p40-1, **37**, **38**, **56**).

The arcade columns in the Gloucester nave surmounted by a triforium also appear at Tewkesbury and it is likely that there was something similar in the Pershore nave. The tall arcade columns

7 Klukas 1983, 304, 309-311.
8 Cox 2010, 35-9.
9 Gem 1986; Guy 1994, 59-64; Fernie 2000, 233-6.
10 Barber 1988, 603; Fernie 2000, 159.
11 Above p62; Gem 1978, 30-31.
12 Thurlby 1996.

13 *VCH Worcestershire*, 2 (1971), 136, https://www.british-history.ac.uk/vch/worcs/vol2/pp136-143, accessed February 25, 2019. At Pershore the north and south responds of the north-west and south-west crossing piers are plain whilst the other responds have paired half shafts to the inner order.
14 Thurlby 1985a, 50 n35; Thurlby 1985b, 10; Thurlby 2003b.

themselves may be allied to those of the naves of Saint-Philibert at Tournus (Saône-et-Loire), Saint-Savin-sur-Gartempe (Vienne), and Sant' Abbondio, Como. The nature of the relationship between these buildings is not understood but there is probably a common source in Roman architecture. An exemplar might have been extant in Gloucester itself in the late 11th century — the lower section of a Roman column excavated in Westgate street, Gloucester, and now in the foyer of Gloucester Museum, is 1m (3 ft) in diameter and when found in 1971 survived to 2m high — it would have originally been c.9m (30 ft) high.[15]

The west front of St Peter's Gloucester may have had a triumphal arch like that at Tewkesbury (**3**, **91**, above p67) which in its turn could have been inspired by the Hereford bishop's chapel and Charlemagne's palace chapel at Aachen. The three-sided termination to the presbytery arcades at Tewkesbury and Gloucester with alternating square and triangular bays in the ambulatory could also be associated with Aachen and its imitators.[16]

Elsewhere, in the Loire valley, an area often referred to by the French as the cradle of Romanesque architecture, the chevet of Sainte-Croix at Loudun (Vienne), commenced in 1062, provides a number of analogues for the presbytery of St Peter's Gloucester. They share an apse-ambulatory plan with a three-sided apse, large columns and 'Doric' capitals, an ambulatory vault with alternating square and triangular bays, polygonal radiating chapels with a semi-circular interior and three-sided exterior, and a high barrel vault. It may also be significant that Sainte-Croix was founded from Saint-Philibert at Tournus.[17]

In Normandy, there is a three-sided termination to the presbytery apse arcade at Saint-Martin de Broglie (Eure). The polygonal ambulatory wall at St Peter's Gloucester may also be related to Romanesque Le Mont Saint-Michel. The chevet of Le Mont Saint-Michel was rebuilt in the 15th century but excavations have revealed an apse-ambulatory plan of polygonal form without radiating chapels.[18] The transepts at Le Mont Saint-Michel retain their Romanesque form complete with barrel vaults — these make it virtually certain that there was a high vault in the eastern arm of the church. These comparisons may not be specific enough to imply a direct connection between the individual forms at Le Mont Saint-Michel and St Peter's Gloucester; nevertheless the use of a high vault at Le Mont Saint-Michel was unusual at the time and Serlo may have wished to reproduce it at Gloucester. More precisely, the paired and sub-arcuated arcades of the nave triforium at Gloucester are remarkably close to the south nave elevation at Le Mont Saint-Michel[19]. The similarity must indicate that Serlo took a hands-on approach to the design of his new abbey church and that the nave elevation at Gloucester was conceived as part of the original design.

One constructional trait at Gloucester indicates an up-to-date knowledge of Norman building practice, namely the oversailing or false bearing (*porte-à-faux*) in the presbytery elevation (**34**, **38**). This can be clearly seen in the nave of Saint-Étienne at Caen, founded by William, Duke of Normandy, shortly before the Conquest (**122**). At Gloucester, however, the same effect is achieved by offsetting the piers and arches of the gallery arcade and the wall above by 0.4m in comparison to the main arcade below. At both Saint-Étienne and Gloucester the distinction is then emphasized by the use of two orders to the presbytery arcade arches as opposed to three orders in the gallery arcades.

The volute capitals (**7**-**9**), which are used for the columns in the central vessel of Gloucester

15 Hurst 1972, 62-3; Fernie 2000, 164.
16 Kidson 1965, 221.
17 Kidson 1965, 221.
18 *Congrès Archéologique* 1966.
19 Fernie 2000, 93, fig72.

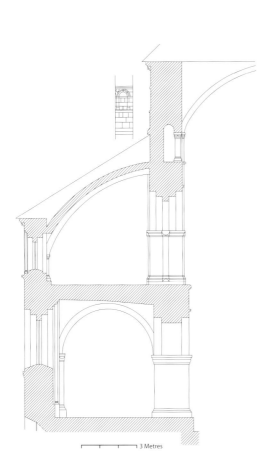

122 Romanesque choir galleries at Gloucester (left, see p29) and Saint-Étienne, Caen (right, model photographed by MT in the Trocadero, Paris), to demonstrate the over-sailing of the first floor. At St Etienne the oversail requires a thickening of the wall of the gallery and above, while at Gloucester the wall is the same thickness in the presbytery and gallery and the over-sail is achieved by offsetting the walls of the gallery 0.4m inside the face of the presbytery.

crypt, and appear on some of the capitals at the west end of the nave north aisle (above **117** E, F), speak of Norman parentage with the closest parallels being at the Benedictine abbey church of Cerisy-la-Forêt (Manche).[20] Similarly, the central placement of the human head on one of the Gloucester crypt capitals (**8**) is paralleled at Cerisy-la-Forêt and Saint-Étienne at Caen. The quadripartite groin vaults in the apses of the north-east and south-east radiating chapels

at Gloucester recall the south transept chapel at Saint-Nicholas, also at Caen.[21]

At Gloucester chevron is used in the arches of the main arcade and triforium, and the jambs of the clerestorey in the nave, whilst it is absent in the presbytery and transepts (except for the reused work on the exterior of the south transept[22]). Such a distribution is contrary to a general principle of Romanesque design in which

20 Baylé 1991.

21 Wilson 1985, 62-3.
22 discussed below pp105-6.

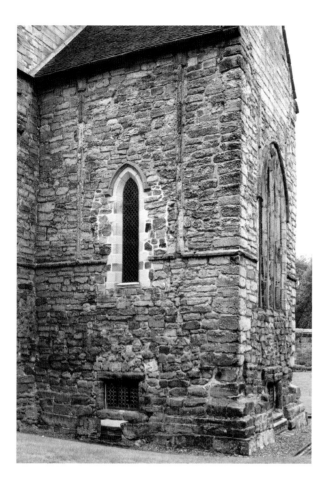

123 Repton, Derbyshire, St Wystan's church, chancel exterior from south-east, showing sill-set pilasters. *MT*

There are some indications of native influences on this otherwise very Norman building.

The arch-within-an-arch of the south nave clerestorey also occurs at the late 11th-century gate tower at Ludlow and is presaged in a MS illustration of the second quarter of the 11th century.[25] Both examples display continuous and non-continuous orders as in the Gloucester ambulatory responds.

At Gloucester the vertical articulation on the exterior of the eastern arm starts at the string course at the windowsill level of the ambulatory and radiating chapels. These 'sill-set shafts' (**39, 40**) are analogous to the exterior of the pre-Conquest chancel at St Wystan, Repton (Derbyshire) (**123**).[26] The absence of capitals on the shafts below the quadrant arches of the presbytery gallery is paralleled in the crossing piers at Stow (Lincs).

The capitals of the north-east chapel of the crypt at St Peter's Gloucester are remarkably similar to those of the chancel arch at St Nicholas, Worth (Sussex) (**124, 125**), a church which may not be Anglo-Saxon in absolute date but which does not include any Norman motifs.

The use of interior hood mouldings in the presbytery gallery arches is an unusual feature not found in English Romanesque architecture until the nave arcades of Malmesbury Abbey;[27] it occurs however over the chancel-arch at Anglo-Saxon Deerhurst (Gloucestershire).

Soffit rolls may also have a pre-Conquest precedent. The arch to the south-east chapel at Deerhurst uses a massive soffit roll,[28] as does the chancel arch at All Saints, Wittering (North-amptonshire). The north and south crossing arches at St John the Evangelist, Milborne Port (Somerset) have soffit rolls whilst the next two orders have quadrant rolls so that the

liturgically more significant parts of a building are more richly articulated.[23] Something similar to the Gloucester arrangement occurs at Durham Cathedral where chevron is introduced in the third bay of the nave main arcade, the second bay of the gallery and the easternmost bay of the clerestorey.[24] In both churches the absence of chevron in the presbytery suggests that use of the ornament was not part of the original design, and that a hall-mark of Serlo's church was austerity of decoration.

23 Thurlby 2012. Its use in Gloucester crypt seems to be an early addition to the original design: above p9-10.
24 Bilson 1922.

25 Thurlby 2006, 40-47, figs 50 and 56; British Library Cotton MS Claudius B iv, fol. 19r.
26 Bony 1981; Taylor and Taylor 1965, figs 556 and 557.
27 Thurlby 2019.
28 Thurlby 2014.

juxtaposition of quadrant rolls and soffit roll is the same as the half shaft and quadrant rolls in the nave aisle responds at Gloucester.[29] Soffit rolls are used in Normandy after 1017 in the presbytery and nave arcades at Bernay abbey and in the crypt at Auxerre and Nevers cathedrals. Pairing of the soffit rolls in the Gloucester nave arcades seems to be a new design introduction though they may be a response to the use of thicker walls.

Two other features could indicate that at least some of the masons were drawing on Anglo-Saxon techniques. In the north transept gallery on the inner order of the enclosing arches the capitals simultaneously form the springer of the arch (**48** inset, **126**). Secondly the Norman

124 Gloucester St Peter's abbey, north-east radiating chapel of the crypt, respond capital. *MT*

125 Worth, Sussex, chancel arch capital. *MT*

126 Inner order engaged shaft with springer carved as scallop capital in the north transept gallery at Gloucester. *MT*

29 Lvovski 2017.

127 Gloucester abbey choir tribune level window of north-east chapel in 2019 after cutting-out of Victorian cement but before repointing. The 'wedge stone springers' produce a segmental arch; they may demonstrate the presence of Anglo-Saxon masons working on the Romanesque abbey in the late 11th century.

windows of the tribune ambulatory level all have 'wedge stone springers' (**127**) rather than traditional springers and voussoirs of Norman construction. These constructional details are unlikely to have been specified by Serlo, and may indicate the practice of indigenous masons.

I have argued elsewhere that scallop and cushion capitals might have Anglo-Saxon origins.[30] However, the immediate inspiration for the cushion capitals at St Peter's Gloucester is likely to be Worcester Cathedral. There, shafts, capitals and abaci in the crypt and eastern slype may have been re-used from an earlier structure,[31] perhaps a building project of Ealdred, who was bishop of Worcester between 1016 and 1062.[32] It should perhaps be emphasised that bishop Ealdred also rebuilt or refurbished the abbey church at Gloucester *c*.1058-60 and this church may have been still standing in 1089,[33] providing inspiration and exemplars for the masons working on the new abbey.

30 Thurlby 2015, 315.

31 Barker 1994, 32; Guy 1994, 24-6; Bryant 2012, 111.
32 Hare 1997, 59.
33 Hare 1993a, 17-20. For discussion of its site and the date of its demolition, *ibid*. 26-9.

SUMMARY

We have created a reconstruction drawing of the Romanesque abbey (**128**), but there are still elements that remain uncertain. The choir in particular presents difficulties. There seems little doubt that it had a stone vault, but it is undecided whether it had a barrel vault without clerestory windows, or a groin vault with them. We are inclined with Fernie (2000, 159) and Thurlby (1985a, 45) to accept that there was a barrel vault (**21, 22C, 37, 38**) and the reconstruction (**128**) shows three small clerestory windows only in the apse. We adopt McAleers suggestion that the high-level passage would have had openings into the interior, like the Tewkesbury and Pershore transepts (McAleer 1986, 168). The question seems to be whether one believes that the east end of a great abbey church would be so dark: the only light would have come from the ambulatory windows of the tribune gallery (if there were any: see above pp30-31), from the choir ambulatory windows and possibly from three clerestory windows in the choir apse. On the other hand, even clerestory windows would have let in very little light (**32B**) especially if they were set into the blind arcading (**32A**), so the presence of a groin vault with such windows (**33, 34**) would not have mitigated the situation very much.

The choir in the Romanesque period would have presented a 'solid' appearance with the emphasis on the horizontal. It is curious that the two eastern piers at tribune level were even more elongated than those below (**17, 18**) — possibly the observer would not have noticed, since the tribune-level arcade was slightly set back from the arcade below.

The 'solid' appearance would have been emphas- ised by the arrangement at the chord of the apse. The triple capital rebuilt into the outside of the north choir (**29, 30**) is massive; given its huge size and thus weight, we cannot believe that it was moved far from its original position. The paired soffit rolls (**31**), on the other hand, need not be from the choir and could derive from one of the transept crossing arches.

Our arguments for a barrel vault in the transepts rely on explaining the presence of the widening-out of the turrets at the top, and it is hard to think of any other explanation for this. The presence of blind arcading on the outside of the transepts (**27, 36**) also seems to suggest a barrel vault, again like those at Tewkesbury (**89**).

As for the north transept clerestory passage (**50**), we are as baffled as anyone: why should the builders not have matched the south side? Did they make a mistake, putting the stair opening too low, and decide to make the best of it?

The decoration of the south transept (**58**) is also a mystery. The plentiful re-used chevron decoration must surely have come from the south transept itself (**67**). The date of the introduction of chevron in England has been thought to be early 12th century (Borg 1967, 129-30) but it may be earlier (Fernie 2000, 176; Moss 2009, 4). The chevron in the crypt (**12, 13**) has been considered in the past to post-date the dedication of *c*.1100, but as we have argued above (pp9-10), the strengthening in the crypt must have become necessary at an early stage; the chevron in the crypt ambulatory vault could thus have been executed well before 1100. The decorated 12th-century transept turrets included chevron stones recut (Bagshaw 2002b, 13, fig16). There is no reason to suppose that there could not have been

128 Reconstruction of the abbey church *c.* 1130. *Drawing: R Bryant.*

chevron before the dedication of 1100. However, if that were the case, then the south transept façade must have been very different from the rest of Serlo's east end; one could not even see it as a principal entrance or façade which would merit special treatment, since the main entrance to the abbey was from the west. On the whole we think that Wilson's assertion that the south transept was rebuilt in the 12th century carries some weight: there is evidence (above p44-7) for continuing late 11th early 12th century problems of stability which could have prompted a mid-12th century rebuild.

The T-mouldings on the north transept (p38, **52**) could be late 11th century; since they seem to be without parallel, they cannot be dated.

As for the nave, the giant pillars may look impressive today (**72**), but they were even more so, 8.4 metres to the underside of the capitals, when first complete: the floor has been raised and bases added since then (**69**).

Our reconstruction of the plan of the west end (**3**, **92**, **97**) relies on Tewkesbury for its design. We are fairly sure that Gloucester had twin western towers. However the monumental western entranceway is by no means certain. It is rendered slightly more likely because there may have been an influence from Hereford, where the bishop's chapel apparently had such an entrance (above p99). However, whatever the design the western entrance at Gloucester abbey would in all likelihood have had several orders, and these would have been elaborately decorated. Hints of such decoration survive on the capitals of the western north aisle respond columns (**117** E-G), and on some of the sculptural material, both in the stone store (**117** H; **118** C-L) and in the building (**116**). If Gloucester was truly an influential centre of carving, it is evident that a great deal has been lost with the demolition of the west end.

BIBLIOGRAPHY

ABBREVIATIONS

Arch J Archaeological Journal

Ant J Antiquaries Journal

BAACT British Archaeological Association Conference Transactions

FGCAR Friends of Gloucester Cathedral Annual Report

GCAR Gloucester Cathedral Archaeological Reports [citations use the site number: major reports will be found on-line at www.bgas.org.uk/publicat-ions/gcar].

JBAA Journal of the British Archaeological Association.

JSAH Journal of the Society of Architectural Historians

PSANS Proceedings of the Somerset Archaeological and Natural History Society

TBGAS Transactions of the Bristol and Gloucestershire Archaeological Society

TWAS Transactions of the Worcestershire Archaeological Society

WANHS Wiltshire Archaeological and Natural History Magazine

BIBLIOGRAPHY

Ashwell, B J 1985 'Gloucester cathedral, the south transept: a 14th century conservation project' *Ant J* 45, 112-120.

Bagshaw, S 2000 'Archaeological recording at the south-east end of Gloucester cathedral' (GCAR 2000/F).

Bagshaw, S 2002a 'The south clerestory of the nave of Gloucester cathedral: archaeological recording in 2001' (GCAR 2001/F).

Bagshaw, S 2002b 'The south transept of Gloucester cathedral, 2002-3: archaeological recording' (GCAR 2002/C).

Barber, W 1988 'History of the monastery of St Peter of Gloucester translated from the Gloucester Cathedral copy' in Welander 1991, 597-639.

Barker, P 1994 *A short architectural history of Worcester Cathedral* (Worcester)

Barker, P and Romain, C 2001 *Worcester Cathedral: a short history* (Logaston)

Baylé, M 1991 *Les origines et les premiers developements de la sculpture romane en Normandie: Art de Basse-Normandie*, no. 100 (Caen).

Baylé, M ed. 1997. *L'architecture normande au moyen age*, 2 vols (Caen).

Bilson, J 1922. 'Durham cathedral: the chronology of its vaults', *Arch J* 89, 101-160.

Bonnor, T 1796 *Perspective itinerary of England: Part 1* (London)

Bony, J 1981. 'Durham et la tradition saxonne', Études d'art medievale offertes à Louis Grodecki (Paris), 79-92.

Borg, A 1967 'The development of chevron orna-ment' *JBAA* 3rd S 30, 122-140

Britton, J 1829 *The History and Antiquities of the Abbey and Cathedral Church of Gloucester* (London). Plates by H Ansted, W H Bartlett and J Carter.

Bryant, R 2012 *Corpus of Anglo-Saxon Stone Sculpture vol. 10: The Western Midlands* (Oxford)

Bryant, R M 2017 'A carved Romanesque springer with voussoirs in Church House, Gloucester cathedral' *JBAA* 170, 180-195.

Carter, J and Basire, J 1807 *Plans, Elevations Sections and Specimens of the Architecture of the Cathedral Church of Gloucester* (Society of Antiquaries, London).

Chowojko E and Thurlby M 1997 'Gloucester and the Herefordshire School' *JBAA* 150, 17-26, Pls III-VIII.

Cox, D 2010 'Evesham Abbey: the Romanesque church', *JBAA* 163, 24-71.

Engel, U 2007 *Worcester Cathedral: an architectural history* (Chichester).

Fernie, E 2000 *The Architecture of Norman England* (Oxford).

Fernie, E 2014 *Romanesque Architecture: the first style of the European age* (New Haven and London).

Gem, R 1978 'Bishop Wulfstan II and the Roman-esque cathedral church of Worcester,' *Medieval Art and Architecture at Worcester Cathedral, BAACT* 1, 15-37.

Gem, R 1981 'The Romanesque rebuilding of Westminster abbey', *Anglo-Norman Studies*, ns 3, 33-60.

Gem, R 1982 'The significance of the 11th-century rebuilding of Christ Church and St Augustine's Canterbury, in the development of Romanesque architecture',: *Medieval Art and Architecture at Canterbury before 1220, BAACT* 5, 1-19.

Gem, R 1986 'The bishop's chapel at Hereford: the roles of patron and craftsmen', in *Art and Patronage in the English Romanesque* (ed S Macready and F H Thompson), London, 87-96.

Gem, R 1988 'The English parish church in the 11th and early 12th centuries: a great rebuilding?', in Blair, J (ed) *Minsters and Parish Churches: The Local Church in Transition 950-1200* (Oxford), 21-30.

Gem, R 1990 'The Romanesque architecture of Old St Paul's cathedral and its 11th-century context', *BAACT* 10*, London,* 47-63.

Guy, C 1994 'Excavations at Worcester cathedral 1981-1991' *TWAS* 3rd S 14, 1-73

Haines, H 1867 *A Guide to the Cathedral Church of Gloucester* (London).

Hamilton, S 2011, 'Edward II and the abbey transformed' in Thomson *et al* 2011, 26-45.

Hare M 1993a *The two Anglo-Saxon minsters of Gloucester*, Deerhurst Lecture 1992

Hare M 1993b 'The chronicle of Gregory of Caerwent: a preliminary account' *Glevensis* 27, 42-4.

Hare, M 1997 'Kings, crowns and festivals: the origins of Gloucester as a royal ceremonial centre', *TBGAS* 115, 41-78.

Hare, M 2002 'Gloucester Abbey, the First Crusade and Robert Curthose' *FGCAR* 66, 13-17.

Hart, W H (ed) 1863 *Historia et Cartularium Monasterii Scti Petri Gloucestriae,* vol 1.

Heighway C M 1993 'Excavations and observation of the late medieval reredos in the south-east ambulatory chapel Gloucester Cathedral' *Glevensis* 27, 21-5.

Heighway, C M 1999 'Gloucester Cathedral south transept and south choir elevations 1999' (GCAR 99/A and 99/B).

Heighway, C M 2003 'Gloucester Cathedral and precinct: an archaeological assessment' 3rd edition 2003 (GCAR OAA).

Heighway, C M 2007a 'Gloucester Cathedral north transept, north-east turret: an archaeological report on works to the north-east transept turret and spire 2006-7 (GCAR 2006/F).

Heighway C M 2007b 'Gloucester Cathedral north transept, phase 2, north gable, archaeological report 2007' (GCAR 2007/A).

Heighway C M 2007c 'Gloucester Cathedral in 1855: the first ever quinquennial' in J Bettey (ed) *Archives & Local History in Bristol & Gloucestershire,* Bristol and Gloucestershire Archaeological Society

Heighway, C M 2008 'Reading the stones: archaeological recording at Gloucester Cathedral' *TBGAS* 126, 11-30.

Heighway, C M 2012 *Gloucester Cathedral south aisle: archaeological recording 1996 to 2012* (GCAR 98/F) (Past Historic).

Hoey, L 1989 'The design of Romanesque clerestories with wall passages in Normandy and England', *Gesta* 28, 78-101.

Hope, St John 1897, 'Notes on the Benedictine abbey of St Peter Gloucester', *Records of Gloucester Cathedral,* vol 3 (1885-97), 90-131. [Also published in *Arch J* 54, 77-119].

Hoyle, D 2011, 'The cathedral foundation', in Thomson *et al* 2011, 47-65.

Hurst, H 1972 'Excavations at Gloucester, 1968-1971: first interim report' *Ant J* 52, 24-69.

Kidson, P 1965 'Gloucester Cathedral', *Arch J*, 122, 221-222

King, J 1986 'Possible West Country influences on twelfth-century architecture and its decoration in Normandy before 1150' *JBAA* 139 (1), 22-39.

Klukas, A W 1983 'Altaria superioria: the function and significance of the tribune-chapel in Anglo-Norman Romanesque: a problem in the relationship of liturgical requirements and architectural form' PhD dissertation, University of Pittsburgh (1978), Ann Arbor, MI.

Luxford, J M 2005 *The Art and Architecture of English Benedictine Monasteries, 1300-1540: a patronage history* (Woodbridge).

Lvovski, R 2017 'Anglo-Saxon or Norman? The church of St John the Evangelist, Milborne Port', *PSANHS* 160, 57-80.

Massé, H J L J 1898 *The Cathedral Church of Gloucester* (London: Bells Guide)

McAleer, J P 1986 'Some re-used Romanesque material in the choir tribune at Gloucester cathedral' *TBGAS* 104, 157- 174.

McAleer, J P, 1984 *The Romanesque Church Façade in Britain* (New York and London).

Meyer, R 1997 *Frühmittelalteliche Kapitelle und Kämpfer in Deutschland*, 2 vols. (Berlin).

Moir, A 2018 'Dendrochronological analysis of oak timbers from the abbot's chapel and Church House roofs, Gloucester Cathedral, Gloucestershire, England' (unpublished report).

Morris, R K 2003 'Master masons at Gloucester cathedral in the 14th century' *Friends of Gloucester Cathedral Annual Report 67 [for 2003]*, 10-18.

Morris, R K 2004 'Gloucester Cathedral Inventory: Category 17: Catalogue of Loose Worked Stones' (unpublished typescript).

Morriss, R K 2002 'Gloucester Cathedral: rapid building survey of the cathedral precincts' (Mercian Heritage Series no 146: report annexed to the Cathedral Conservation Plan).

Morriss, R K 2017 'Recent excavations at Gloucester Cathedral' *Glevensis* 50, 30-36.

Moss, R 2009 *Romanesque Chevron Ornament: the language of British, Norman and Irish sculpture in the twelfth century* BAR International Series 1908.

Mychalysin, P 2007 'Appendix 1: archaeological and petrological survey of the north transept north elevation' in Heighway 2007b, 15-17.

Phillips, D 1985 *The Cathedral of Archbishop Thomas of Bayeux: excavations at York Minster* vol 2 (HMSO).

Rowell, R L 2000 'The archaeology of late monastic hospitality' unpublished D Phil Thesis, University of York, Dept of Archaeology, September 2000: Chapter 5: Gloucester Cathedral.

Taylor, H M and Taylor, J 1965 *Anglo-Saxon Architecture* vols 1-3 (Cambridge).

Thomson, Celia *et al* 2011 *Gloucester Cathedral — Faith, Art and Architecture: 1000 years* (London).

Thurlby, M 1985a 'The elevations of the Romanesque abbey churches of St Mary at Tewkesbury and St Peter at Gloucester' in *BAA CT* 1985, 36-51.

Thurlby, M 1985b 'The Romanesque elevations of Tewkesbury and Pershore' *JSAH* 44, 5-17

Thurlby, M 1996 'The abbey church, Pershore: an architectural history', *TWAS*, 3rd Ser 15 (1996), 146-209.

Thurlby, M 2003 'The Norman church' in R K Morris and R Shoesmith (eds) *Tewkesbury Abbey History Art and Architecture* (Logaston), 89-108.

Thurlby, M 2006 *Romanesque Architecture and Sculpture in Wales* (Logaston).

Thurlby, M 2012 'Articulation as an expression of function in Romanesque architecture', in *Architecture and Interpretation: Essays for Eric Fernie*, ed. J A Franklin, T A Heslop and C Anderson (Woodbridge), 42-59.

Thurlby, M 2014 *The architecture of Deerhurst priory: The 11th- 12th- and early 13th-century work* (Deerhurst).

Thurlby, M 2015 'The Anglo-Saxon tradition in post-Conquest architecture and sculpture', in *The Long Twelfth-Century View of the Anglo-Saxon Past*, ed. D A Woodman and M Brett (Farnham), 307-58.

Thurlby, M 2019 'The Romanesque abbey church of Malmesbury: patronage and date', *WANHS* 112, 236-64

Toulmin-Smith, L (ed.) *The Itinerary of John Leland* (London 1907-1910).

Tristram, E W 1944 *English Medieval Wall Painting: the twelfth century* (London)

Waller, F S 1856 *General Architectural Description of the Cathedral Church…at Gloucester* (London).

Waller, F S 1876 'The crypt of Gloucester Cathedral' *TBGAS* 1, 147-152.

Waller, F S 1890 *Notes and Sketches of Gloucester Cathedral.*

Waller, F W 1911 'Gloucester Cathedral tower' *TBGAS* 34, 13-194.

Welander, D 1991 *The History, Art and Architecture of Gloucester Cathedral* (Gloucester).

Whitelock, D (ed) 1962 *Anglo-Saxon Chronicle* (London).

Wilson, C 1980 'The origins of the Perpendicular style and its development to *c.* 1360' PhD thesis, Courtauld Institute, University of London, December 1979, registered 1980.

Wilson, C 1985 'Abbot Serlo's church at Gloucester (1089-1100); its place in Romanesque architecture' in *BAACT* 7, 52-83.